Guerrilla Tourism Marketing

Increase Your Profit by Leveraging Marketing, Technology and Relationships

by Carol Wain
and
Jay Conrad Levinson

ISBN: 9781482035636

Published by: WINning Entrepreneur Press, a division of World Incentive Network Inc.

Promotion by: Marquee Marketing, a division of World Incentive Network Inc.

Cover Design by: Kayla Curry

Author Bio

Carol Wain, President of World Incentive Network (WIN) and "2003 Entrepreneur of the Year", is a coach, consultant, trainer and globally renowned business improvement and marketing specialist who teaches and helps successful entrepreneurs, professionals and experts to leverage what they already have: expertise, relationships and resources to increase their business and personal success.

Carol has a long history in multiple areas of tourism including: incentive travel planner, event planner, travel agent, ski resort supervisor, front desk clerk, night auditor, restaurant manager and waitress. For more information visit http://carolwain.com

Jay Conrad Levinson, Father of Guerrilla Marketing, is the author of the best-selling marketing series in history, *"Guerrilla Marketing."* His books have sold more than 20 million copies worldwide and have influenced marketing so much that they appear in 62 languages. Today, Guerrilla Marketing is most powerful brand in the history of marketing, listed among the 100 best business books ever written, and is a popular website at www.gmarketing.com.

This book is dedicated to entrepreneurs who never give up even when others have given up on them.

Contents

Authors' Notes:

Join us on Facebook http://facebook.com/guerrillatourismmarketing

Go to: http://guerrillatourismmarketingbook.com to register your receipt and receive you bonus

Carol Wain Website

If you would like to connect with Carol Wain directly visit her website at http://carolwain.com

---

Guerrilla Tourism Marketing is written for all segments of tourism, however the principles apply to many businesses, so please recommend this book to your friends and family.

Guerrilla Marketing Overview - In this section, the authors outline guerrilla marketing concepts; how to identify your ideal customer so that you speak directly to them; ways to increase customer lifetime value; how to create value differentiators, so price shopping is reduced; which guerrilla marketing weapons work best today; and managing your online reputation to earn more business.

Multi-Channel Marketing - In this section the authors discuss ways to use multiple, digital marketing tools to increase engagement, exposure, traffic and profit. Topics include internet marketing, local marketing, social media marketing, mobile marketing and promotional strategies.

Leveraging Relationships - In this section the reader is introduced to ways to leverage relationships using fusion marketing (joint ventures, strategic alliances); create and nurture relationships by providing exceptional customer experiences; earn customer engagement; build a community around your business; attract and retain guerrilla employees; incentivize key people to encourage desired behavior; and recognize employees to create a more profitable business that delivers on your brand promise and builds more engagement.

Action Time - In this section you will create a plan to increase profit and build and nurture relationships within your business.

Please Review This Book on Amazon

Thank you for buying this book.

We would love to hear from you so that we know what you love and what we could do better in the next edition.

Please go to Amazon and leave a review.

To get more tips, hints and best marketing practices sign up for Carol's newsletter at http://carolwain.com/

Foreword

By Jay Conrad Levinson

The tourism industry is balanced on the edge of a precipitous incline. Literally, it means life or death for the tourism professional -- life for those who are aware of the multiplicity of marketing options for the guerrilla marketer and adios for those who are still clueless as to what to do next.

That depressing news is balanced by the impressive news that there now is a marketing treasury for tourism marketing guerrillas. It's given added heft by the fact that the key to the treasury is in the hands of Carol Wain and that you now have the combination in the pages ahead.

Does this give you an unfair competitive advantage? That's the name of the Guerrilla Tourism marketing game. This is the book that helps you win the game. The truth is that winning the game today is easier than it used to be -- but it's still not easy -- unless you're a marketing guerrilla.

Carol and I know what that takes and we've given in to you in this book -- not every bit of it but enough to make your profits soar even in an ailing economy. In the fool's mind there are many options. In the guerrilla's mind there are few.

Use them to provide for yourself the satisfaction you strive to give to your clients.

Jay Conrad Levinson
The Father of Guerrilla Marketing
Author of the Guerrilla Marketing Series
21 Million Sold; now in 63 languages

Acknowledgements

To my husband Steve Wain, my friend and my love... thank you for putting up with me as I went through the journey of building then rebuilding my business. You have been so patient and supportive and I thank you from the bottom of my heart. To my daughter Lauren, who gives hugs at just the right time, thank you for being the amazing young woman that you are (and for staying out of my way when I was beyond stressed)! To my daughter, Lindsey, who always seemed to call me when I was "busy", thank you for understanding. It's time for another spa day.

To Joyce Collicutt, thank you for reading every word in this manuscript multiple times and for helping me to finish my thoughts, remove extra words and otherwise help me to get my knowledge into a format that makes sense. To Katheryn Coleman, thank you for giving me a "semi-colonoscopy". As I was going through your edits, your humour helped keep me going. For Karen Smith, thank you for your feedback on the manuscript. I took your recommendations to heart and now the "how-to" sections are in the Guerrilla Marketing Workbook. To "Jump Start" Jim, Chianese, thank you for recognizing my talent and for helping me to leverage my book. To my Mom, Yvonne Watt, thank you for reading the manuscript too, it's great having "newbie" eyes reviewing the material to be sure that it makes sense. And finally to my patient graphic designers who competed through 99Designs.com to create my cover.

I also cannot thank my wonderful interviewees for sharing their experiences, knowledge and advice: Sohail Khan, Harris Rosen, Jay Rosenberg, James Schramko, Andreas Schmidt, Dave Smith, Rob Warner and David Zinger.

Finally, to Marie Forleo, you are an incredibly smart, caring and a fun mentor. You helped me to get beyond what I thought I should be doing to the place where I can be authentic, provide the most value and live the life I want. Thank you!

Introduction – The Perfect Storm

"It is not the strongest of the species that survive, nor the most intelligent, but the one most responsive to change."

Charles Darwin

It seems that the tourism industry cannot win for trying some days. Politicians are adding taxes, changing laws and doing whatever they can to make up for lost revenue, often at the expense of business. Markets are shaky, currency fluctuation is making it incredibly difficult to effectively plan and governments are falling like leaves in a storm. Tourism, which is a significant portion of many economies, is particularly susceptible to macro economics, politics and media coverage as decisions about travel, meals and entertainment expenses are made based on how confident we are about spending our discretionary income.

Media and Politicians

For those of us that rely on incentive travel, the future is rather grim as we are the target of both politicians and media. In 2008, American Insurance Group (AIG) was one of the companies bailed out by the Federal Reserve to the tune of $85 billion. Shortly thereafter, the media "exposed"[1] an incentive travel reward for independent insurance agents at the St. Regis Resort Monarch Beach in Dana Point, California. The media and politicians acted like rabid dogs as they reported on this "extravagance", denouncing the program and demanding that heads roll. The so-called "AIG Effect" effectively destroyed the meeting and incentive travel segment of the industry, as corporate leaders decided that it was better to pay the cancellation penalties for incentive travel, meetings and events rather than risk having a journalist plaster their name on the front page of the newspaper for being "irresponsible" with taxpayers or shareholders hard-earned money.

Then on February 11, 2009, President Obama made the following statement "You cannot get corporate jets. You cannot take a trip to Las Vegas or go down to the Super Bowl on the taxpayers' dime.

---

[1] http://www.forbes.com/2010/02/16/aig-business-travel-leadership-meetings-10-corporate-conferences.html

There's got to be some accountability and some responsibility."[2] The intent appears to be a reality check for Wall Street executives with entitlement expectations. That is a solid argument. However, the implications were much greater as the news spread that Obama had said that corporations should not be going to Las Vegas for their meetings, events or incentive travel. The effect was felt throughout the world as other high-profile organizations reigned-in their travel spending. Lay-offs occurred; profits diminished; and many businesses went bankrupt (including the, now-infamous St Regis, which defaulted on its $70 million loan to Citibank and was placed into foreclosure in 2009)[3].

The situation improved somewhat between 2010 and 2012, with incentive travel and meetings making a slow and steady come-back but then another few sucker-punches came our way. During the race for the Presidency, Mitt Romney reminded the good people of Nevada that the President is against tourism in their State[4]. The media continues to report on "excessive" spending on meetings and events, which are fantastic profit generators for host communities and their host hotels, restaurants, ground transportation, production companies and retail shops.

The US Government Services Administration (GSA) held an event in Las Vegas that was contrary to government spending guidelines[5] and is now facing congressional hearings while an Australian bank[6] is being targeted for "extravagance" because of a recognition program held on Silverseas Cruises' *Silver Shadow* shortly after laying-off 1,000 employees. While it appears that the decision makers at the GSA knew that they were in violation when they planned their meeting, the message about the effectiveness of well-planned, measurable incentive programs, corporate meetings and events is not being heard and this is having wide-reaching effects on the travel industry.

---

[2] http://www.huffingtonpost.com/2011/10/24/obama-las-vegas_n_1029134.html
[3] http://articles.latimes.com/2009/jul/21/business/fi-stregis-foreclose21
[4]http://www.politifact.com/truth-o-meter/statements/2012/feb/08/mitt-romney/mitt-romney-says-president-told-people-skip-vegas-/
[5] http://www.incentivemag.com/article.aspx?id=8087
[6] http://meetingsnet.com/corporatemeetingsincentives/news/anz_takes_heat_for_incentive_0223/

Economic Impact

The economy, still a bit shaky, has certainly influenced our buying habits. For restaurateurs, the impact is felt when their customers buy ready-made meals at the grocery store and invite friends over instead of dining out. When customers choose to eat out, they may select a quick service restaurant (QSR) rather than a sit-down option. Interestingly, but not surprisingly, for the first time, more than half of all meals eaten outside the home in the UK[7] are now at QSRs. Restaurants that cater to the corporate market, such as "downtown" restaurants and restaurants in hotels and airports are seeing lower overall spending as the budgets for meals and entertainment are slashed. While the luxury market does not seem to be as impacted because of wealthy customers, the people and businesses that "traded up" to luxury during the boom times are now purchasing at the levels they can afford. For all the ancillary products and services that tourism brings; from cab fares to entertainment and from linens to produce, the impact is just as acute.

Our Customers

Eventually, the politicians will be replaced, the economy will cycle back, journalists will find juicier stories and the purse strings will loosen again. There is one perfect storm factor that is not likely to change though – our customers, who use the internet to research for solutions to their problems and sometimes know more about our products and competitors than we do. Our customers tend to ignore our traditional marketing, primarily because it has lost its reach, and they are increasingly influenced by what they find online. They rely on the recommendations of friends, acquaintances and complete strangers. These customers and potential customers are using their power to influence and it is up to us to adapt and embrace this new reality.

---

[7]   http://www.telegraph.co.uk/finance/newsbysector/retailandconsumer/9016251/Fast-food-becomes-the-UKs-meal-of-choice.html

Fortunately, guerrilla marketing is all about a different reality; one that is based on a foundation of increasing our profit by leveraging our relationships. Guerrilla marketers know how to implement plans to win the war that is attacking them from all sides and I am here to show you how.

Online Reputation Management and Social Presence

Another game changer is the rise of the very public and permanent online reviews and testimonials. Business leaders resent public complaints as they are damaging to their reputation. It is not unusual for a review to blind-side the leadership team because a customer chose to post it online instead of raising their issue with someone who could rectify it. Reviews can also be inaccurate or fabricated by a competitor or disgruntled employee. Unfortunately, it does not matter what circumstances lead to the review being posted because the damage has already started. Unless the leaders show that they are listening and respond appropriately, the impact of negative reviews could result in a loss of business for years.

On the other hand, positive reviews often result in more sales because of the social proof that results from those reviews. I have been in the travel industry since 1996, first as a retail travel agent, now as the owner of an events, marketing and incentive company. Over the years, I have connected with many representatives from Convention and Visitor Bureaus (CVBs), Destination Management Companies (DMCs), hotels, cruise lines and tour operators. I also have an extensive network of travel agent and planner friends but instead of reaching out to anyone I know most of my personal travel purchase decisions are based on the reviews I find on TripAdvisor and other review sites. I will explore reputation and review management later in this book

Embracing Change

As leaders, we need to take a good long look at our businesses and what we can do to leverage our relationships to increase profit. There are many factors that contribute to success and failure. Some are outside of your control, like over-zealous politicians or journalists on a mission, a pandemic, weather or an economic meltdown. However, there are many factors that are within your control. It is up to you to determine how to plan and implement change to make you stronger; and this book is designed to give you the insight and tools to help.

Guerrilla Tourism Marketing will investigate ways to improve your profit, engage your customers and leverage your employees using guerrilla marketing techniques, multi-channel marketing tools and community building, along with performance improvement and engagement strategies. I will give you examples of things that work and things that do not work. I will give you exercises and ask questions designed to help you become very clear on your marketing and what how to improve your business (I created a handy Guerrilla Marketing Workbook, which contains these exercises, along with checklists and detailed how-to information, which can be purchased by following the link at http://carolwain.com.) What I will not do is recommend anything that is going to cost you an arm and a leg. After all, guerrilla marketing is not about huge budgets, it is about inspiration, imagination, preparation and implementation.

Let the journey begin...

Part One –
Guerrilla Marketing

In this section we explore ways to use guerrilla marketing concepts, guerrilla marketing weapons and marketing basics to increase your profitable sales and create long-lasting relationships that you should leverage.

Chapter 1 - Guerrilla Marketing Overview

"Marketing is not an event, but a process . . . It has a beginning, a middle, but never an end, for it is a process. You improve it, perfect it, change it, even pause it but you never stop it completely."
Jay Conrad Levinson

Let us start by understanding what guerrilla marketing is all about. For those of you who have read other guerrilla marketing books, this will be a review... with a twist. After all, guerrilla marketers know that creativity, skills and experience are valuable weapons. I have taken our creativity, skills and experience to create our own version, which can be used by all businesses while being specifically targeted to our tourism industry.

Guerrilla Marketing is:

- The connection between you and whoever buys what you sell;
- All contact that anybody has with your business/organization;
- Truth made fascinating;
- Your chance to educate your market to succeed with their goals;
- A process of small details such as cleanliness, neatness, clothing and how the phone is answered or people are greeted;
- Consistency in every touch point with a customer;
- All about knowing and focusing on customers and "How will they feel after they make the purchase from me?"
- Not complicated;
- A chance to achieve success using unconventional means and creativity;
- Techniques and strategies that do not cost a fortune. Instead you invest your time, energy, imagination and knowledge;
- A conversation where you create relationships by asking questions and asking permission rather than broadcasting a monologue;
- Mastering the art of listening then solving the problem and selling the solution;
- "You" marketing rather than "Me" marketing. It is all about the customer; and

- A plan that you commit to.

Guerrilla Marketing Concepts Include:

- Measuring profits and relationships, not hits, sales, traffic or other metrics;
- Using psychology and human behavior rather than guesswork;
- Maintaining your focus on your core business while adding more excellence to what you offer;
- Growing geometrically by enlarging the size of the transaction; increasing the number of transactions each customer has each year; and creating a referral network in addition to marketing;
- Looking for organizations you can cooperate with. These companies share the same standards and customers as you do;
- Sharing and giving to make the lives of your customers better: give first – ask later;
- Creating marketing combinations which work the best, rather than single actions or activities; and
- Aiming your marketing at individuals or extremely small groups rather than general / mass marketing.

These concepts are brilliant, powerful and doable. The bottom line is that every single person that works with your business is in marketing: from the leaders and managers within the organization, to the back-office, front-office and never-ever-seen people… each and every one of you is in marketing. The concept is simple but it is more difficult to get your employees to understand this. I will get into the topic of guerrilla employees later in this book, however, for now it is important for you to understand that every touch point that your customers, potential customers and influencers have with your business is "marketing". If your employees are sloppy in their appearance; or there is garbage on the floor; the table cloth is stained; the call center representative is not quite as friendly as expected; your ad has a typo; or your employees are talking to each other instead of helping guests you will experience lower profit and weaker relationships because you have failed to provide a positive customer experience. However, the employee's impact on your business does not end after his shift ends. Employees talk about your business with friends and family in casual conversation and they could also be talking about your business online. The impact of their conversations and actions outside of work is just as impactful, if not more so, because instead of talking to one, two or even a few people, they are talking to hundreds, thousands or tens of thousands of people, depending on the platform.

The expectations for how employees interact with people should extend beyond the workplace to include strict rules about representing the company when they are away from work. Employees need to understand why these rules are in place and the impact that they have when they speak of or post about the business. Since there are differences across jurisdictions for employer and employee rights, check with your legal team, and/or your human resources team for the regulations and precedents for policies relating to opinion and content shared online outside of work hours. Finally, understand, and instill in your employees, that you are all in this together – you are all part of the success, or failure, of your business.

Consider This:

You are the owner of a DMC and your marketing message says "We make you look great", which is important to your target audience, the meeting planner. However, most established DMCs have a message that says "We can make you look great", in one form or another because they have friendly staff, they are creative, they have many local connections and they can pull rabbits out of hats, if needed.

To make the truth fascinating you would grab a portion of your competitive advantage and Unique Selling Proposition (USP) and make it fascinating. For example, I spoke with the owner of a Latin American DMC and he told me that all of his staff is annually trained in first aid because many of their client events occur in the jungle. I found that statement to be interesting but not particularly incredible… until he told me why… ambulances could not reach many of the events for over an hour. Even helicopters may not have easy access, so it was extremely important to have everyone on staff trained as a first responder in case of injury, illness or medical emergency. Now that is fascinating.

Continuous Activity

Too often business owners, particularly smaller businesses such as independent hotels, B&Bs, spas, golf courses, restaurants and tour companies forget that marketing is continuous and it needs to be measured, split-tested and adjusted. Many times they make the mistake of thinking that placing advertisements in the local paper, on the radio, or in the Yellow Pages is marketing. It is not. It is a component of marketing, one that is not very effective for most businesses, but it is not marketing. Instead marketing is so much more. It includes:

- Your relationships;
- The experience you provide to your customers;
- Your knowledge;
- Your communication channels;
- Your message;
- Your brand promise; and
- Your campaigns.

Purchasing Decision Making

As you will read in the Guerrilla Selling Chapter, there are four personality types who have different needs and expectations for receiving information that helps them to make a purchase. When you tweak with your marketing and selling to match their personality you will sell more.

People make their purchasing decisions based on emotion and justify their decision using logic. People also picture themselves using, benefiting and/or enjoying a product and/or service before they make a decision to buy. They put themselves into the scenario that you create in your marketing campaigns and judge whether it will work for them or not. They imagine themselves in the playground that you create for your business.

You need to ensure that you appeal to both emotion and logic with your marketing message because approximately half the population is left-brained. They are logical, sequential reasoners who love facts and numbers and words that explain things. The other half are right-brained and they respond to aesthetic and emotional stimulation through their senses with colors, images, sounds, smells and tastes.

As you are considering the various marketing campaigns and activities and strategies, if you do not include numbers, lists and words that explain the logic and why they should buy from you, you will lose your left-brained audience. If you do not use pictures and other elements that evoke emotion and appeal to the imagination, you will lose your right-brained people. Be sure to include elements that appeal to both types of customers.

Target Market and Target Audience

Let us start by identifying each as the terms are often used interchangeably. Your target audience is the people at the receiving end of your marketing messages and they either influence or make the purchase decision and your target market is the people that will buy your product or service.

McDonald's and Disney understand the parents are the target market but the children are the target audience because children influence their parents to buy the McHappy Meal or take them to Disneyland. I will explain the role of influencers later in this book.

Your "A" List and Your "B" List

The Pareto Principle[8] states that eighty percent of effect results from twenty percent of cause. You will likely find that eighty percent of your sales come from twenty percent of your customers; profit comes from twenty percent of customers; problems come from twenty percent of customers; and referrals come from twenty percent of customers.

 To use this principle to maximize your profit and to better leverage your relationships with customers, divide your customers into groups.

As Jay says "treat your "B" list like royalty and your "A" list like family", so pay special attention to your "A" and your "B" list. I would like to add, treat everyone well it is good for business – besides you never know how influential they are.

Your "A" list is comprised of your highly profitable, easy to please, frequent buyers that are advocates for you and your brand. You do not want to risk losing them to your competition directly or through the influence of others. Your "B" list customers buy from you but they are not necessarily your best customer. They may be infrequent buyers; may ask for discounts; may only shop for sale items or with coupons or on an industry rate; or may be a bit more demanding in terms of support.

---

[8] http://en.wikipedia.org/wiki/Pareto_principle

A Word of Caution

Your customers that are not-profitable and/or cause the most problems are your "F" list clients and they need to be either given a warning or simply fired. It is never easy to do but guerrillas recognize they only have so many resources and subsequently cannot concentrate on finding more "A" list clients if their lives are made difficult with "F" list clients.

Sometimes your "F" list clients simply need a warning to change the dynamics in your relationship. People will push boundaries and see what they can get away with, so it is your job to enforce collaborative conditions.

A friend told me about two customers who were nasty to his staff. They were verbally abusive for the slightest mistakes. He would not tolerate the attack on his staff so he told both customers that they must change the way they communicate. One customer apologized, the other was indignant. "Mr. Indignant" was promptly fired, which increased moral.

I have fired a few clients over the years and some of them have been annoyed that I let them go. However, I was always relieved and new opportunities always present themselves. Besides, it is always fun to think of what ex-clients are doing to our competition.

Guerrilla Marketing Tip for Quick Profit

I interviewed James Schramko who had worked his way up the ranks to become a General Manager at a Mercedes-Benz dealership prior to founding SuperFastBusiness in Sidney, Australia. (The interview can be found at http://carolwain.com). I asked him what he would do to increase profits quickly, he responded,

> *"I would firstly look at historical data. I would take the last 12 months and I would find out everything that has been sold and find out where those customers came from. Why did they buy? My first tip would be to do more of that because a lot of them overlook that one basic thing. Almost every business can benefit from this today. Just look at what is actually been happening. We have that data right in front of us.*
>
> *My parents had a travel agency so I have actually done this. We found out most of their profit was coming from businesses*

with five to ten people, not too big, not too small and these people wanted to simply pay to have everything handled for them. I said, 'Go and get more customers just like that and zoom in on your best customer and zoom out from your worst customer,' so identify who your best customers are.

In the Mercedes-Benz dealership we did the same thing and we called it a matrix. We would map out everything we sold and the profit we made and we were able to find our sweet spot. We knew that there was a certain product range that sold really well all of the time, had the best customer and the most profit and then there were some that we almost always lost money on so we just avoided them."

What is your fastest path to cash? Who are the people that you can target easiest to bring in the most profit in the least amount of time? How can you reach them this week?

Chapter 2: Creating Your Ideal Customer Avatar

"The aim of marketing is to know and understand the customer so well the product or service fits him and sells itself."

Peter Drucker

Throughout this book, I ask questions and suggest exercises designed to help you to better understand how to maximize your profit and leverage relationships. All these exercises, along with checklists and more detailed how-to information are included in the Guerrilla Marketing Workbook, which can be purchased separately at http://carolwain.com

Knowing your target market and target audience is the first step for crafting your marketing message for maximum impact. However, groups of people do not buy from you – individuals do – and the next step is to create an ideal customer avatar that represents the best customers for your products, services and vision for your business.

This is perhaps the toughest exercise that I undertook when I reinvented my business. I had completed Guerrilla Intensive – the 3-day guerrilla marketing training facilitated by Jay – and I thought that I had identified our ideal customer at that time. I created products and services deemed valuable by this customer and I started to implement my marketing plan. However, when I repeated the exercise as a student in Marie Forleo's B-School I realized I had it all wrong. I originally chose an ideal customer based on emotion rather than on my core strengths and my ability to make the biggest impact in their lives. It was not easy to accept that I was positioning my business for the wrong customer but in situations like this, I recall the Turkish proverb "No matter how far you have gone on a wrong road, turn back".

Defining Your Ideal Customer Avatar

The purpose of this exercise is to help you to determine who your ideal customer is and how to market to him/her in the words that will resonate. Your goal is to understand this person so well that you can anticipate his/her needs thus creating a long and profitable relationship.

To figure out your ideal customer avatar think about your best customers and what they have in common. Think about the demographics (age, income, marital status, family status, industry, gender, race, home ownership, employment status etc.) and psychographics (values, beliefs, interests, hobbies etc.). Note that you may have multiple ideal target markets for your business, so think about your ideal customers for each of your products and services.

For example, if you own a golf resort, perhaps you have an:

- Ideal golf club member;
- Ideal local market single round golfer;
- Ideal mid-week guest;
- Ideal weekend guest;
- Ideal lunchtime restaurant customer;
- Ideal dinner restaurant customer;
- Ideal customer for the ballroom; and
- Ideal customer for the meeting space.

Take some time and define each and every one of your ideal customer avatars. You need to be so analytical and studied you practically assimilate the customer and anticipate his needs.

While you are doing this exercise, have some fun and really "make" this person. If you have heard of The Sims, a video game where you can create your people and control their lives, this is what you want to do here. You will want to know things such as:

- Name (make one up);
- Age;
- Gender;
- Hair and eye color;
- Marital status;
- Does he have children? How many? What ages? What are their names?
- Where is his residence? Owned? Rented? Which neighborhood?
- How much does he make? What is the combined family income?
- What is his occupation?
- What are his hobbies?

- What are his favorite books, movies, music, TV shows, magazines, blogs and YouTube videos?
- Does he travel for work? How often?
- Where does he travel on vacation?
- Does he own a cottage? A trailer? A 5th wheel? A boat?
- What kind of car does he drive?
- Does he ride a motorcycle?
- What is his favorite meal? Favorite drink?
- What are his guilty pleasures?
- What clothes does he wear?
- Does he wear glasses?
- Is he friendly and outgoing or reserved and professional?
- Does he curse?
- Are there any other descriptors that match your ideal customer? If so, include them.

I recommend finding an image of your ideal customer avatar along with images that represent the other components of his life that you have identified above. Make a mini scrapbook of your ideal customer, so that you can visualize him as you create your campaigns.

Frank Kern talks about his experience with one of his ideal customers. He was on his way to a conference to speak about internet marketing and he created an ideal customer called "Bob" who is 45 years old, sells insurance, is married and has two kids who drive him nuts. Bob's wife thinks he is crazy for buying all this "internet stuff" from scam artists. He is 25lb overweight, wears glasses, khaki pants, white button shirt and brown leather shoes. His biggest desire is to quit his $48,000/year job but his biggest problem is that he does not know where to start and he gets overwhelmed with all the information out there. After his presentation a man approached Frank ... his name was Bob, he was wearing khaki pants, white shirt and brown leather shoes (no glasses). He was married but his kids did not drive him crazy and he made $45,000 per year. Bob bought Frank's product and continued to buy stuff from him because Frank was talking specifically to Bob in his marketing materials. That is how powerful this exercise can be.

Diving Deep into the Minds of Your Ideal Customers

Now let us try to get inside the head of this person. This is a little harder to do but it is extremely important to understand so do not skip this step. You might find that you are not keen on doing this but it can make the difference between success and failure with your marketing messages. It was during this part of the ideal customer exercise that I realized that I had the wrong ideal customer in mind. Dig deep and do the hard work to get a clear picture of your ideal customer.

Tip: if you have difficulties with some of this, ask someone who represents your ideal customer. It is not cheating – in fact it validates your beliefs and it helps you to understand this person better. I give full credit to Marie Forleo for teaching me how to do this and for insisting that I do not skip this step.

Thinking as Your Ideal Customer:

- What do you worry about?
- What is keeping you up at night?
- What is your worst case scenario?
- What is your true situation? (as opposed to the one that you present to the world)
- What would people think if they knew your true story?
- How could your situation get worse than it is now?
- How could it get worse than the worst case scenario?
- What would happen if things do not improve?
- What would you pay almost any amount for to help you change your situation and/or avoid the worst case scenario?
- If you found that dream solution, what specific changes would it make to your life now and your future?

I know it seems like a lot of effort to get inside the head of your ideal customer but if you do not put yourself firmly in his shoes, how will you know what to say to get him to buy from you? If you cannot answer those questions, then you do not know your ideal customer well enough to speak to him, in the language that he understands, with offers that he will buy.

You might be thinking "I sell pizza. Why do I need to know if my ideal customer is about to lose his job, his wife is having an affair and his house is about to be repossessed?" It is important because he may not currently buy from you because he has a well paying job and he is living a good life. However, when he is forced to move into a bachelor pad, while he is looking for work and dealing with his marital situation, your message about how your take-out pizza not only fills him up but provides great nutrition at a fraction of the cost of dining out might be just what it takes to get him to call you.

By the time you have finished this exercise, you will know a lot more about how to position your brand, your products and services to your ideal customer. Your copywriting, promotions and marketing tools will be so much easier and you will have more success than a buy-one-get-one (BOGO) offer that you thought might work.

What are Your Customer's Dreams?

Guerrillas use their imagination to determine the desires and dreams of their ideal customer, while connecting those dreams and desires to their products and services – you would be wise to follow this example. Do not sensor yourself, just let your mind come up with some ideas and record, type or write them down. Consider that there are surface desires and there are the core desires. For example, the ideal customer's surface desire could be to eat out without worrying about his food allergies. His core desire is to be able to relax and enjoy himself, knowing that his concerns are addressed and he can enjoy his meal.

A meeting planner's surface desire could be that she wants to be awarded a contract based on creative use of a budget. Her core desire is to have her suppliers provide incredibly creative ideas, cost-saving suggestions and a promise of outstanding on-site support, in addition to achieving her budgetary desire.

As your ideal customer, answer the following question: "If I could just…" Record your responses. Are there any fantasies that you can deliver? If so, highlight them. Are there any fantasies that you would be willing and able to deliver? Give those ideas a big star. Can you charge a premium for any of these? Give those ones a happy face. What other ways can you help your ideal customer right now?

You could be tempted to skip these exercises but do not because the insight that you will uncover will make a huge difference to the success of your marketing and your business. You are outlining what your ideal customer looks like, what his fears, desires and true situation is so that you can market to him in a way that resonates with him. It helps you to clarify if you really want "this person" to buy from you. It also helps you to determine how valuable you will become to him because you know exactly what he is going through and what he needs.

A mentor used to constantly remind me that "what I focus on grows", so if you focus on what you want – an ideal customer who loves you because you enrich his life in ways he could not imagine, who refers you to his friends, who is a brand advocate, who appreciates your staff and who forgives the occasional hiccup that he may experience – you may just find that customer gravitating to you in ways you could never imagine.

Chapter 3 – Defining Your Value Story

"If you do not have a competitive advantage, do not compete."
Jack Welch

We all risk turning our businesses into a commodity that is price shopped because potential and current customers cannot differentiate between us and our competition. Therefore, to avoid being commoditized, you need to explain your value. In this chapter I am going to explain ways to maximize your profit while adding the value that your ideal customers will gladly pay for.

Creating New Market Space

You can increase your value by breaking all the rules and by doing something completely different – not thinking outside of the box – but throwing that box and all preconceived notions away. In the book, Blue Ocean Strategy[9], authors W. Chan Kim and Renée Mauborgne, explain how to create uncontested market space and how to make the competition irrelevant. It is a fantastic book and I highly recommend it as you will more thoroughly understand the concepts of a Blue Ocean Strategy and how to execute it properly. For the purposes of this book, however, here is a highly condensed version.

Cirque du Soleil is one of the examples of how a visionary entrepreneur created an entirely new concept. Is it a circus? Theater? Acrobatics? A production show? In fact, Cirque du Soleil created entertainment that had not existed before – a circus that appeals to adults; that sells at a high price point; does not use animals; incorporates a story line and theme; features acrobatic performances with an original score; performs in unique venues and has a high-production value. Guy Laliberté, the CEO of Cirque du Soleil turned the concept of a circus, which was a declining industry, on its head and into a brand new form of entertainment that borrowed from theater, ballet and Broadway to create this unique type of circus entertainment. Kim and Mauborgne call this "creating a blue ocean" which differs from the "red ocean" full of bloodshed (and low margins) of a highly competitive marketplace.

---

[9] http://www.blueoceanstrategy.com/

To summarize their approach, the first step is to take a look at what your industry values. You start by looking at what you currently offer and eliminate parts that do not add value to your customers. You also look at the factors that should be reduced well below the industry standard. Then you create new factors that the industry has never offered and finally you look at the factors that you can raise well beyond the industry standard.

Eliminate, Reduce, Raise and Create: The case of Cirque du Soleil:[10]

Eliminate	Raise
Star performers Animals Concession sales in the aisles Multiple show arenas	Unique venues
Reduce	**Create**
Fun and humor Thrill and Danger	A Theme Refined Environment Multiple productions Artistic music and dance

After you define the "Create", "Eliminate", "Reduce" and "Raise" factors that you can use in your own business to create a blue ocean strategy, then plot it on a strategy canvas such as the one on the next page.

---

[10] Blue Ocean Strategy Book Page 36

Strategy Canvas of Cirque du Soleil[11]

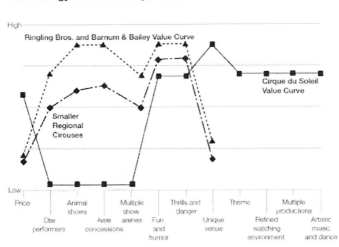

The Strategy Canvas of Cirque du Soleil

When you look at what Cirque du Soleil did in the strategy canvas, the concept becomes clearer. You will see how they all but ignored the components of a traditional circus while keeping "Fun and Humor" and "Thrills and Danger" and then adding components that were new to a circus.

Pret a Manger, a UK fast food chain, incorporated a number of unique concepts when it opened in 1998[12]. Pret knew that its customer base of business people was concerned about healthy eating; prompt service and reasonable prices and traditional fast food restaurants were not offering all three. So their concept, which is still used today, is to offer premade soups, salads, sandwiches, sushi and desserts made fresh in their in-store kitchens throughout the day. Pret uses the highest quality ingredients and sells them in a supermarket-type atmosphere. All meals that are unsold at the end of each day are donated to charity. Pret does not make custom meals or provide food service. Instead their customers enter the store, choose their meal and go to the cashier, which is a complete change to the line-up, place your order, pay, get your food routine that other QSRs use. The

---

[11] Blue Ocean Strategy Book Page 40
[12] Blue Ocean Strategy Book Page 105 - 106

average customer spends 90 seconds from the time he has chosen his meal to the time he leaves the store.

When I created my incentive travel business in 1996 I approached my business model in a unique way too. I had no preconceived notions about what I should or should not be doing because I did not know the industry fully enough to know these types of businesses even existed.

The traditional businesses in the incentive market were large, with many sales people, who sold through relationship building and wined/dined their Fortune 500 customers. The biggest businesses in the industry had sprawling campuses, which meant lots of resources, lots of people and lots of overhead.

I created a small, lean business – Incentive Depot, now known as Marquee Incentives – that operates without in-house sales people, relies on its website for finding new customers and caters to smaller organizations with programs deemed to be too small for its competition. The mission is simple – do whatever it takes to impress clients and their participants and add value by providing more reward options, more services and more ways to help clients achieve their goals. The Marquee team goes out of its way to understand client challenges; to be an extension of their in-house team; and to make the decision maker look good. One of the differentiators is that program managers are empowered to "go shopping" to find a reward elsewhere if it cannot be sourced from current vendors so the participants are not inconvenienced as a result of a back-order. The focus on making the participants happy results in positive reviews, testimonials and letters of appreciation from participants, their bosses and the program managers. Because the Marquee team gets to know clients' program managers by proving it cares about them as individuals, their participants, objectives and challenges Marquee is able to renew contracts easily. One client, who did not fit the profile of being "too small for the competition", shared that she was regularly approached by sales people from the bigger incentive companies but they did not get very far because she did not want to deal with anyone else.

When I started my business I was not a brilliant strategist; I was a military wife and mother to two small girls so necessity, honestly, contributed to creative and strategic thinking. As my business evolved it became "that small town merchant" that knew its customers' likes, dislikes and situation, even though the customers were not local and were, in fact, spread across Canada, the USA and Mexico. Although, the Blue Ocean Strategy was not written when I created my business, I used the authors' concept to show how I created my business in 1996.

Eliminate, Reduce, Raise and Create: Marquee Incentives

Eliminate	Reduce
Cold calling	Cost of sales
In-person pitches	Overhead
Trade show booths, magazine ads	Research expenses
	Organizational hierarchy
Responding to Requests for Proposals	
Paper reward catalogs	
Large campuses	
Raise	**Create**
One-to-one relationships	An effective website
Innovation	Unique packages for rewards
Creating "Wow" moments	A "family"
Flexibility	Software to manage incentive programs

Consider your business. What can you eliminate, create, reduce or raise so that you do not compete head-to-head in a highly competitive market? Additionally, what values can you emphasize that will bring you more profit?

Specific Value Creators

There are certain aspects a business can focus on to carve out its own niche within a crowded marketplace and add value for its customers. The following examples reflect my experiences. I would love to hear your thoughts, so please visit my blog at http://carolwain.com or connect with me on any of the social networking sites we both visit to share them.

Better service

- My family cruised with Celebrity Cruises a few years ago. While the food quality and service in the main dining room were perfectly acceptable and included in our cruise fare, we tried the specialty dining room because our sales representative told us how great it was. Even though there was an additional per person cover charge, we booked it and after the exceptional service and fantastic meals, we promptly booked it again for the last night of our cruise. So, offer better service and it will result in higher revenues.

Empowered Employees

- My husband, Steve, and I have experienced empowered employees as a guest at Casa Velas in Puerto Vallarta. Our concierge, Gabrielle, recognized that due to a food allergy, I would not be able to enjoy dining at their beach club, so she offered me the option to order from the regular resort menu and she arranged for the meal to be prepared at the beach club so that I could dine there with my husband. Empowered employees immediately attend to your customers' needs, which in turn heighten the experience and ultimately increases repeat and referral business.

Reliability

- I am always reluctant to book any tour operator that reserves the right to make discretionary changes to a package or charter flight. A few years ago, there was a tour operator/airline that flew into our local airport on a weekly winter charter to Mexico. For reasons that I suspect were purely financial, the operator pulled the flights part way through the season, expecting their booked passengers to travel approximately six hours, including a ferry ride, to Vancouver. A story in the local paper highlighted the plight of a father who was originally scheduled to fly to his daughter's wedding on one of the cancelled flights. With the schedule change, he would miss his daughter's wedding. There is sometimes an extra price to be paid for reliability, which translates into higher profits and delighted customers.

Corporate Stability

- When I book group travel for a meeting or incentive years in advance, I absolutely want to know that the vendors will all still be in business during the event. Therefore, I examine my vendors closely, looking at factors such as how financially secure they currently are and how well they are engaging their customers before I choose one vendor over the other. Corporate stability equals higher profits, equals more corporate stability.

Quality

- When I was growing up I often heard "You get what you pay for" in terms of the cost of something versus its quality. There are cheap products that are made cheaply; expensive products that are made cheaply; and inexpensive products that have a quality that is better than expected. It bothers me when I order a $15 hamburger that started out as a frozen patty. For $15 I expect a burger that is made with fresh ground beef right there in the restaurant instead of being served a patty I could buy from a warehouse store. On the other hand, when I pay for something with a lower price point and the quality exceeds my expectations, I feel like I have won the lottery. Exceeding quality expectations means happy customers and higher profits.

Prestige

- Club floors, airport lounges, private dining rooms, first-class, and to-die-for hotels and restaurants are all examples of ways to justify your value. Give people a reason to "tell their friends" and they will. In my role, I admit, I am offered wonderful upgrades that most people do not receive and I do love it. I also pay for upgrades to the club floor or to a private dining room and I share my experiences with my friends, who then consider upgrading to have that same experience and those bragging rights. Owners of restaurants, clubs and pubs know that being the "hot spot" in town means better margins, so consider the prestige factor as part of your plan. People like to feel special and will spend more for this feeling.

Reputation

- Hand in hand with prestige, your glowing reputation will command higher profits as customers expect to pay premium prices. You can use your great reputation in many ways. Depending on your brand promise (ensuring that you live up to it) and as you attract raving fans, your prices can increase, along with your profits. As a sidebar, you can be instrumental in building your reputation through social and mobile marketing in ways that were never possible before and many of the tools are free or low-cost.

Products from Socially Responsible Companies

- Condé Nast Traveler has annual awards for tourism businesses that give back to their communities, hire locals, build schools, buy locally, buy carbon credits, etc. None of the winners that I have ever read about are in the value category of lodging or tours. People will pay more to support businesses that give back because it helps them to justify their purchase.

Social Proof

- People who are looking for a place to dine will skip the empty restaurant in favor of the full one. My friend, Joyce, experienced this first hand at a pizza restaurant in Seattle. It was a large, empty restaurant but her family was hungry and they decided to go in for convenience. The service was poor and the food was disappointing, which Joyce shared when she "checked-in" to the restaurant on her smart phone. The next night they found a Mexican restaurant two blocks away from their hotel, which was pulling out tables from storage because they were so busy. They decided to eat there and had a fantastic meal. I will provide more information on social proof later in this book because it is so easy to optimize for profits.

Exclusivity

- Sponsors of group incentive travel programs pay for exclusive events and experiences that their qualifiers would not/could not do on their own. This adds to the "wow" factor of the reward;
- I am always thrilled when I get an invite to exclusive events and exclusive areas of a venue with my VIP access and have been known to occasionally flaunt my great fortune on social media. Exclusivity is an extremely valuable way to increase profits.

Knowledgeable Employees

- We have all experienced that uncomfortable situation where a front desk clerk, waiter, sales representative or another front-line employee is unable to answer a fairly standard question. While on a site inspection to the Marriott World Center in Orlando, the sales manager told our group that the woman who was leading our inspection knew everything about the property. If any of our group could stump her, she would have to drink a shot of tequila. We were challenged to listen to what she was saying and to come up with questions that she could not answer. It was a fun inspection and a smart man in our group, Jason, managed to stump her with "How many hang points are there in the ballroom ceiling?" Before we left the inspection we had the answer, although she was still required to have that shot. What this experience showed us is that this team is fun and knowledgeable. We know that we can ask them anything and they can tell us promptly, which makes the meeting planner look good, which is a valuable feature to remember.

Caring Employees

- A few years ago I was on an Amadeus Waterways cruise in Europe with Steve and our youngest daughter. Cruise director, Peter, was not only incredibly fun and funny but he went out of his way to ensure that everyone was taken care of. When Steve lost a crown on his tooth, Peter went far beyond what we expected, even offering to arrange a visit to the dentist in our next port. While Steve did not take him up on his offer – opting to wait until we returned home – we share this story with anyone who is contemplating a river cruise in Europe.

- My daughter asked that I highlight another cruise employee, a bartender from Royal Caribbean International, who became her "best friend" on the ship. We were travelling together on a mother-daughter cruise for her eighth birthday. Lauren still remembers how Markus made her a special drink (Sprite with grenadine) each time she visited the Solarium. She was so touched that we shopped in two ports for a gift for him and when she presented it with a hand-made thank you card, we all ended up in tears. This bartender made her trip memorable and we did our part by writing a wonderful letter of appreciation. Shortly after we returned home, we received an email from Markus thanking us for our letter, which was read to all the staff and which resulted in a promotion for him.

- In 2011, my family went to Sheraton Universal City for a couple of days as part of a San Diego / Los Angeles trip. Sadly, we had a death in the family while we were there. When I was checking out, the front desk clerk asked how everything was, which is expected. When I choked back my tears to tell him of our family tragedy he went beyond the normal "Oh, I am so sorry for your loss", to ask how we were doing and whether I was close to my mother-in-law. He asked if there was anything he could do for us and then extended an invitation to return again so he could personally ensure an enjoyable return visit.
- We would gladly go back and stay with any of those companies because of their exceptional service. It is all about the experience that the guests receive and a customer will pay extra for that.

Consistency

- Consistency is hard to achieve. Even companies like McDonald's (I was an assistant manager for two years) who are all about consistency with step-by-step guidelines, secret-shoppers, checklists and extensive training are still inconsistent. It can simply come down to who is working on any given day.
- Some companies focus more on demanding a consistent experience for their customers and they reap the rewards by being able to deliver on that promise.
- There are very few places that receive my business because they are consistent but the Westin Wall Centre in Richmond, BC is one such place. I know each and every time that I stay there that the service will be similar; the room will be as I expect and my stay will meet my expectations. The Marriott chain is another one of my favorites when travelling to unknown destinations because I know what to expect. Demand consistency which ensures a positive customer experience and then find ways to charge more.

Customization

- Starbucks is the master of customization. We get exactly what we ask for and pay a premium for it. Also, no matter where you travel in the world, you will likely find a Starbucks, although the company is customizing the experience based on the expectation of the clientele.
- In our room in Le Blanc Spa and Resort, Cancun, Steve and I had a bath menu, a pillow menu and a wine menu and if we did not like the Bulgari toiletries, we could order another brand. Combined with our butler – who could arrange nearly anything – and the sommelier – who produced fantastic wines that were not on the menu – the premium that we paid was well worth it. Customization to exceed customer expectations allows your business to charge a premium, which results in higher profits.

Delivery

- Dominos Pizza guarantees thirty minute delivery or your order is free. Are they the lowest cost pizza place in town? No but they can charge more because of their brand promise.
- Our local pubs and restaurants took a one-two punch with the introduction of a new sales tax and a reduction in the tolerance for blood-alcohol-levels in drivers. The smart establishments "delivered" people to their businesses and then back home again. What did it cost them? Only the rental of a mini-bus, driver and gas that they shared.
- When you remove the barriers of delivery, however they exist; you can charge a premium and increase profits while delighting your customers.

Availability

How can you make yourself or your staff or your product more available to your customers? Our customers expect 24/7 availability and while it is not always possible to give that type of service personally, you can find creative ways through   call centers / answering services to always be available in one capacity or the other.

- My group coaching clients have access to me through their membership website and through other social media groups such as LinkedIn and Facebook. Our marketing and incentive program clients are given my mobile phone for emergencies. In the past, I gave them my home phone number but we no longer have a home phone. I was very reluctant to give out my home phone number to my clients for fear that they would abuse the privilege but no-one ever did. I believe it was because my team took care of them during our typical work week, as well as by answering questions that they had via email outside of work hours. Therefore, there was no need to call... but knowing that they could, was valuable to them. This personal service gives an added piece of mind and leaves a lasting impression while creating value for our clients.

Flexibility

- At my business, we are so flexible that no two incentive programs have been identical. The services are offered à la carte and billing is unique to each client. This does create additional work on our behalf but we provide exactly what the client wants ... and then some. All requests are considered and my staff either implements immediately or provides a quote to the client within two days. This approach impresses our customers, enhances our products and services and results in repeat and referral business.

Environmentally Friendly

- This is a sore point for me. If I am at a conference or tradeshow I can be in my room for as little as four hours a day. I often travel by myself and I do not need my sheets changed nightly. I can also use my towel more than once. Many properties claim to be eco-friendly, yet they still change the sheets or replace hanging towels, so they are not living up to their environmentally-friendly promise. Personally, I prefer staying at properties that will not change the sheets unless you leave the "card" on the bed as the onus is on me to remember to put the card on the bed if I want clean sheets. Being environmentally friendly reduces expenses while it connects you on an emotional level to your customers.

Locally Sourced Products

- Locally sourced products offer many advantages. Food products, particularly perishable products, taste better when they are naturally ripened when compared to produce that was picked days or weeks prior. Customers will happily pay more for fresh, tasty local produce.

- There are many restaurants and hotels that source local produce. However, one of our local restaurants, namely a restaurant called "Locals" goes beyond the competition by not only buying local for a significant portion of their menu but by listing the business names and owners on its website. Buy local, support your community and increase your profits.

Amenities

- Never underestimate the power of amenities as they make a huge difference to the experience of your customers/guests.
- Restrooms at restaurants, hotels, lounges, clubs and pubs that are stocked with amenities add to the overall experience. In fact, clean bathrooms with appealing décor and amenities are an indicator of the value of a business as it impacts the customer's overall experience.
- I love great amenities in my guest room and I will choose one property over another for amenities, all things being comparable. You can increase your price by using the extras to impress your customers and ultimately increase your profits.

Selection

- Having a large selection is important to the overall experience. My family does not often travel to the same resort more than once but we have been to Sandals Ocho Rios and Beaches Turks and Caicos twice because of the selection of room types, room amenities, dining options, wines, mini bar selections, activities and spa treatments, in addition to the other "wow" factors such as great service, fun atmosphere and caring employees. Take a look at ways you can increase your selection while increasing your profit.

Activities

- In tourism, activities are a key differentiator between competitors, primarily for resort hotels, tour operators, cruises and incentive travel programs. The more exclusive, the more adventurous and unique the experience, the more you can charge as it gives your guests more options to satisfy their needs.

Entertainment / Fun Factor

- Dining at Señor Frogs is more than just eating a meal in a restaurant – it is an experience. The waiters engage guests with funny name-badge stickers, hats and funny signs. Is Señor Frogs inexpensive? Was the food the most amazing thing I have ever tasted? No, but they know that they serve up a good time that is worth a premium. They keep you there longer by entertaining you and thereby increasing the per-person spending, which increases their profits.

Brand Name

- Often in tourism, businesses that are part of a franchise or chain can "coast" on their brand recognition easier than the independent brands. In many cases, this brand recognition allows for premium pricing. Part of that is the consistency factor: part quality, part reputation and meeting customer expectations.
- As I mentioned above, Señor Frogs, along with many other franchise restaurants can charge more than independents who may even be better in terms of the overall customer experience. But, if you are an independent business rather than a franchise establishment do not fret, I will give you some equalizing ideas later in this book.

Comfort

- It goes without saying, if your guests do not sleep well, get burned in the shower or lose circulation in their legs on an excursion due to uncomfortable seats, you will never be able to charge a premium. Do not ever discount the comfort factor. If you have a product offers more comfort than your competitor, even if that is one of the few competitive advantages you have, promote it constantly. Those of us who are spending our discretionary dollars on tourism experiences will pay more for comfort and we will share this with our friends and family.

I have given you a number of ways to define your value story and carve out a niche that maximizes your profit. Consider using these ideas as a framework for enhancing the experience for your ideal customer.

Chapter 4 – Increasing Customer Lifetime Value

"The purpose of a business is to create a customer, and to grow that customer."

Peter Drucker

There are multiple ways to increase your revenue including increasing targeted traffic to your website or location in addition to converting more traffic and prospects to customers. You can also increase Customer Lifetime Value (CLV) by convincing customers to spend more on each transaction, increasing the frequency of purchases and by ensuring the relationship continues well beyond the first transaction. Guerrillas know that companies can boost profits by almost 100 percent by retaining just 5 percent[13] more of their customers. Ask yourself, "How much does the average customer spend in a year? How many years can I retain them? How often do they buy (timeframe)? How much do they spend a month, per transaction?

Number Crunching Time

Let us say I own a restaurant and Joe spends an average of $25 once every three months ($25 x 4 = $100) over a five year period. The average CLV would be $100 each year x 5 years = $500. If I wanted to increase my existing customer sales by fifty percent I could focus my efforts on enticing Joe to:

- Increase his spending with a higher average check per visit;
- Dine at my restaurant often; or
- Keep Joe coming for more years.

I could increase CLV by fifty percent in any of the following ways:

- Convince him to spend an average of $37.50 each visit = $37.50 x 4 visits per year x 5 years = $750
- Entice him to dine with me every two months, instead of three months = $25 x 6 visits per year x 5 years = $750; or
- I could work on deepening our relationship so that he continues to buy from me for 7 ½ years = $25 x 3 visits per year x 7.5 years = $750

---

[13] http://hbr.org/1990/09/zero-defections-quality-comes-to-services/ar/1

To increase CLV I would use a combination of guerrilla marketing weapons (which I explain in detail in the next chapter) such as a birthday VIP club, a customer appreciation event, a "bring a friend" promotion and text message blasts with a "dine today" promotion. If I could encourage him to dine 7 times a year and spend $30 each time and he remains a customer for 6 years his CLV would increase to $1,260, which is a 252 percent increase. Imagine what these types of increases would do for your business.

Now that you can see the power of increasing CLV here are some guerrilla insights for doing so:

Reduce Churn

If you own a hotel and the average guest stayed one night, once a year, what would It be worth to have them stay two nights each year? What about the situation where a guest visits your destination every year but your hotel is not always the chosen hotel. What would it be worth for you to always earn their travel dollars?

I went to the Motivation Show in Chicago every year for about ten years. I spent three nights each visit and not once did a hotel representative ever ask me if I would like them to make a reservation for me for the next year's stay. So, instead, each year, I looked at the negotiated rates, checked the internet and made a decision based on emotional factors (for example one hotel had quieter rooms, breakfast was included at that property etc.) along with the room rate. During the Motivation Show Chicago hotels are pricey, so it really does boil down to my mood. Even though the hoteliers expect that they will be at full occupancy, they are leaving money on the table because they do not know how many other trips I make to Chicago each year. Consider what would happen if someone contacted each of the guests from the previous trade show, six-months in advance of the next show, to ask if they could make a reservation for them? What if they also asked if the guest had any other trips planned and, if so, would the guest like to make that reservation now too?

The guest may think that you consider her to be a valued customer and she could be extremely grateful for the effort made to make their business travel planning easier. Even if the guest has someone else handling her travel arrangements (for example, an assistant or the corporate travel desk), what impression would be left with the guest that you just contacted? This simple, yet effective way to increase your CLV also creates an exceptional customer experience because your employees do something that your competition does not do: they offer a personal touch and they wow the guests with a higher level of customer service.

Increase Frequency

Perhaps your business is a golf course and you know that certain members only ever golf when you offer a promotion for twilight golf. What if you called, emailed or sent a text message to this segment of customers informing them about the next promotion before it was made public and offered them the chance to book a tee-time in advance? Do you think that perhaps they might golf more often? Do you think they could arrange for one, two or three more golfers to join them if you gave them two days to arrange it? This low cost, personal touch increases your profits by ensuring enhanced golfers' experiences, which in turn results in an increase in CLV.

If you are a meeting planner and you book one event for a client each year, is it possible to book two events? You may be planning a sales retreat/conference for the client but can you add their customer appreciation event? You never know until you ask. Offer an incentive to encourage clients to book their second event through you as well.

Build Relationships

In each of these scenarios you are building a relationship with your customers, by being helpful, building trust, creating rapport, adding value and increasing your profit because you have done something that your competitors do not do, you have recognized your customers as individuals.

I absolutely love going to the Black Fin pub in Comox, BC because my favorite waitress, Maggie, knows what I like to order when I am there. When she sees me enter the pub, she greets me and asks if it will be the usual. Maggie knows her customers and goes above and beyond to remember their names and their preferences, which delights customers by making them feel valued and important. If I owned this restaurant, I would ensure that all my staff followed Maggie's lead as it is a low cost way to increase customer engagement and, in turn, CLV.

Increase Commitment

Increase your CLV by increasing your customers' commitment to return. If you own a resort spa, are you asking your clients to book their next appointment before they leave? If not, you are missing the opportunity to increase the number of times they will visit in a year and you may lose them to a competitor that does ask. You are doing your customers a favor by blocking the space for them the next time they need a service while removing the possibility that you will be booked up when they call at a later date. My manicurist is great at doing this but the other spas that I frequent do not, which means that each time I need a service I call around to see who can accommodate my schedule. If the receptionist always offered to book my next appointment at the time I paid for the service, not only would it save me time and possibly disappointment but it also greatly increases the chance that I will visit that spa the next time. Restaurants that require reservations can ask their customers if they would like to book their next "date night" or "get-together"; travel agents can ask if there are any more trips that they can book; meetings planners can ask about a repeat event; and destination representatives and event venues can ask for the opportunity to host the next meeting. When you ask at the point of sale you are asking for a commitment when the customer is in a buying mood and it is more likely to result in a return visit.

Upselling

An increase in CLV can be achieved by upselling, which is a sales technique used to persuade or influence a customer to purchase an upgrade or other add-ons. You would not believe the number of times I asked "Is that a large Coke?" when I was an assistant manager at McDonald's. If a person typically spends $20 with you, how can you make it $22 or more? Suggest a balcony instead of an ocean view cabin; a pre or post tour extension; a golf and meal special; the luxury car instead of the midsize; or, as I experienced at Señor Frogs, "Do you want the "girl-size", the "man-size" or the "vacation" size cerveza?" That was a brilliant upsell which we were drawn to for emotional reasons. After all, Steve is not going to order the "girl-size" and I am not going to order the "man-size"… not when there is a "vacation-size" available.

To use upselling effectively, it is important that you create a script and ensure that absolutely every one of your employees follows it.

Consistency is extremely important from an experiential perspective and from a profit perspective.

Cross-Selling

A similar sales technique is cross-selling where you would offer related products to customers when they make a purchase. "Would you like fries with that?" was my cross-selling question at McDonald's. Amazon is great at cross-selling too because they display a "Customers who bought this item (what you just bought) also bought these items." Related products for a trip could include travel insurance, a coupon book or event tickets, or a sleeve of golf balls at a golf course. A savvy travel agent could partner with a house-sitter, pet-sitter, cab company and clothing store and cross-sell those services.

Discount airlines seem to have perfected the cross-sell. They know that they cannot make money with a 99 pence or $15 base ticket price, so after you have decided to buy a ticket from them, the cross-selling and upselling opportunities are mind-boggling. In addition to the advanced seat selection, preferred boarding, checked luggage "option" and meal vouchers (which are upsells) the next series of options are for partner offers. Do you need a car? Hotel? Bus? Attraction tickets? The cross-selling continues during your flight too. Do you need ear-phones? A blanket? Food? Drinks? An air-sickness bag?... okay, I just made that last one up... but the point is that the airlines make a lot more profit from you when they sell you these items than they make if you only purchase a ticket.

As advisors and trainers working with entrepreneurs to increase profitable sales by leveraging relationships, there are many ways that we can increase the CLV of our customers, while, at the same time, giving them the best possible combination of products and services to help them achieve their objectives. If we are retained to create and manage an incentive program to increase sales, we can also offer our services to find fusion marketing partners and create a compelling offer to further increase sales. If we identify that they are also having trouble connecting with customers and prospects, we will offer to help build a community around their business to engage those people. If we hear that they have a challenge in an area that is not our core business, we will recommend someone who can help them. Our motivation is simple... the more value we provide to our clients, the longer they will retain us and the more they will spend. On the other side, the more value we provide to our clients, the more successful they will become, which makes them happy and we are there to celebrate in their success.

The best part about cross-selling, assuming that you are properly cross-selling items that your customer values, is a well received, successful suggestion. Think about your shopping experiences for a moment: If someone asks you if you need batteries for the toy you are buying, or if you need a car rental when you have just booked a flight are you not grateful for the suggestion as it will save you time, effort and, maybe even, money?

So always think in terms of a win-win situation. Your customers win because they have a more complete experience or product for their problem and you win because you have increased your sales, added more value and added to your goodwill account.

Offer After a Purchase

Guerrillas are always on the lookout for ways to increase their profit and nurture relationships. One way that they can do both is by offering a special one-time-offer (OTO) to the customer. Online, after you have made a purchase, you may see a message on the thank you / confirmation page that looks something similar to "Thank you for your purchase. As a valued customer, we have a very special offer for you" "This offer is not available anywhere else, nor will it be offered again, so go ahead and add to your cart." The concept of a one-time-offer is similar to a cross-sell but the difference is that it truly is an exclusive offer that will not be made available again.

If you use this technique, you are capturing people when they are in a buying mood and they are more likely to respond to a great offer. Instead of having a boring "thank you" page on your website, use this valuable real estate to increase your profit.

The one-time-offer can be used at your location too, although unless you have a very strict script which you enforce, you will find that some employees comply and others do not. Even the employees that do comply will have different success rates in selling the OTO. To aid with compliance, be sure that your staff can see the relationship between what they are selling and the OTO and why it benefits the customer, themselves and the business.

Follow-up

Guerrillas know that the power is in follow-up after the sale to ensure that everything went as the customer expected. You will stand out in the minds of your customers because you are doing something that most businesses fail to do.

For example, after a round of golf your employees could offer help and ask "How was your game? Oh, that is too bad; would you like to join us for a lesson? We have a special promotion." A front desk clerk should always ask how the stay was during check-out but a customer-care representative can follow-up a day or so later to ask for specific feedback such as what the guest liked and what could be improved. A restaurant manager could call, email or text customers the next day to ensure that their meal experience was positive. A spa director could contact the guest to receive feedback on the treatment. Each time that a personal connection is made with a customer, ensuring they were happy with their experience, you solidify your relationship with them. So create a follow-up plan for your business that outlines what action will be taken by whom, what they will do and when it will be done.

Increasing your CLV is one of the ways to increase profit, so consider the ways to increase it in your business.

Chapter 5 – Guerrilla Marketing Weapons

"Half the money I spend on advertising is wasted; the trouble is I do not know which half".

John Wannamaker

Guerrilla marketing is not about having the biggest budgets or the largest marketing department; it is about achieving success using unconventional means. Guerrilla marketing is not complicated but it is about being creative, patient and strategic while using certain guerrilla marketing "weapons" to achieve your goals. Jay created his first list of guerrilla marketing weapons many years ago and I have updated them. Some of these weapons will work for you, others will not, as every business is different. Technology continues to change and I will revisit this list for additions and deletions from time to time. You can check out http://carolwain.com for the most current list.

200 Guerrilla Marketing Weapons

1. Your marketing plan(s)
2. A marketing calendar
3. Your brand identity
4. Business cards
5. Stationery (digital and print)
6. Personal letters
7. Telephone marketing
8. A toll-free number
9. A vanity phone number
10. The Yellow Pages
11. Postcards
12. Classified ads
13. Free ads in shoppers
14. Per-order and per-inquiry advertising
15. Circulars and flyers
16. Community bulletin boards
17. Magnetic and vinyl car signs

101. Your employees and reps
102. A designated guerrilla
103. Employee attire
104. Your social demeanor
105. Your target audience
106. Your circle of influence
107. Your "Hellos" and "Goodbyes"
108. Your listening skills
109. Your teaching ability
110. Your community-building ability
111. Sales training
112. Stories
113. Networking
114. Professional titles
115. Affiliate marketing
116. Media contacts
117. "A-List" customers

18. Movie ads

19. Outside signs

20. Street banners

21. A window display

22. Inside signs

23. Posters

24. Door-to-door canvassing

25. Door hangers

26. An elevator pitch

27. A value story

28. Upsells and cross-sells

29. Letters of recommendation

30. Attendance at trade shows

31. Direct mail

32. Television commercials

33. Newspaper ads

34. Radio spots

35. Magazine ads

36. Billboards

37. Online directories

38. Craigslist, Kijiji

39. Digital business card

40. Social media accounts

41. Check-in services accounts

42. Mobile / smart phone

43. List building (email / direct mail)

44. Personalized email

45. An effective email signature

46. Mobile website

47. Mobile applications (apps)

48. Video email

118. Your core story

119. A sense of urgency, scarcity

120. Limited time or quantity offers

121. A call-to-action

122. Satisfied customers

123. A benefits list

124. Competitive advantages

125. Exceptional customer experiences

126. Multi-channel marketing

127. Public relations

128. Fusion marketing

129. Barter/contra

130. Word-of-mouth

131. Buzz

132. Community involvement

133. Club and association memberships

134. Promotional products / swag

135. A tradeshow booth

136. Special events

137. Memorable name tag

138. Luxury box at events

139. Gift certificates

140. Audio-visual aids

141. Advertising

142. Reprints and blowups of magazine ads

143. Coupons

144. A free trial offer

145. Guarantees

146. Contests and sweepstakes

147. Baking or crafts ability (for gifting)

148. Lead buying

49. Videos posted to YouTube
50. A corporate website
51. A geo-niche website
52. A landing / squeeze page
53. A merchant account
54. Ecommerce enabled website
55. Auto-responders
56. Good search engine ranking
57. RSS feeds
58. Blogs
59. Podcasting
60. Online Reviews
61. Links from social bookmarking sites
62. e-Books
63. Content creation
64. Webinars
65. Joint ventures
66. Word-of-mouse
67. Viral marketing
68. eBay and other auction sites
69. Click analyzers
70. Pay-per-click ads
71. Money keywords
72. Google Adwords
73. Sponsored links
74. Reciprocal link exchanges
75. Banner exchanges
76. Website conversion rates
77. Electronic brochures
78. Google+ Local pages
79. Specific customer data
80. Case studies
81. Sharing
82. Brochures
83. Catalogs

149. Follow-up
150. A tracking plan
151. Marketing-on-hold
152. Branded entertainment
153. Product placement
154. Being a radio talk show guest
155. Being a TV talk show guest
156. Crowd-sourcing
157. A proper view of marketing
158. Brand name awareness
159. Intelligent positioning
160. Knowledge of your market
161. A meme

162. A theme line
163. Writing ability
164. Copywriting ability
165. Headline copy talent
166. Location
167. Hours of operation
168. Days of operation
169. Credit card acceptance
170. Financing availability
171. Credibility
172. Reputation
173. Efficiency
174. Quality
175. Service
176. Selection
177. Price
178. Upgrade opportunities
179. Referral program
180. Spying
181. Testimonials
182. Extra value
183. Adopting a noble cause

84. White papers
85. Public service Announcements
86. A newsletter
87. Speeches
88. Free consultations
89. Free demonstrations
90. Free seminars
91. Articles
92. Columns
93. Writing books
94. Publishing-on-demand
95. Workshops
96. Tele-seminars
97. Infomercials
98. Constant learning
99. Marketing insight
100. Yourself

184. Easy to do business with
185. Honest interest in people
186. Good telephone demeanor
187. Passion and enthusiasm
188. Sensitivity
189. Patience
190. Flexibility
191. Generosity
192. Self-confidence
193. Neatness
194. Aggressiveness
195. Competitiveness
196. High energy
197. Speed
198. Focus
199. Attention to details
200. Ability to take action

Which of these weapons can you use with to communicate your value, your blue ocean strategy and your unique selling proposition to your ideal customers?

Traditional Guerrilla Marketing Weapons:

Yellow Pages

With the transition to internet-based local search, customers are becoming less and less likely to use the Yellow Pages; not only because of the convenience and speed of the internet but they are also looking for reliable sources for reviews and other information about the companies they are considering, which is not possible with print advertising.

Yellow Page providers realize that they need to do something to keep from becoming extinct. One of the solutions they have attempted is internet-based Yellow Page directories. These directories work much like the printed version. Your ad is placed in the applicable business category on the assumption that people will use those directories to find local businesses. However, the reality is that those sites have very little traffic - Google, Bing and Yahoo are the places that people most often turn to when they are looking for local businesses.

In San Francisco, David Chiu from the San Francisco Board of Supervisors has proposed an ordinance[14] that bans the Yellow Pages for automatic door-drop. His reasons are:

- San Francisco receives almost 1.6 million Yellow Pages phone books each year, even though there are only about 800,000 residents. Like junk mail and spam, many of the phone books are unwanted and never get used.
- At an average of 4.33 pounds per book, the Yellow Pages create nearly 7 million pounds of waste every year in San Francisco.
- Based on disposal and recycling rates, the hidden costs of phone books in the waste stream may be over $1 million per year.
- A fifty percent reduction of Yellow Pages produced for San Francisco residents would save nearly 6,180 metric tons of carbon dioxide emissions annually.
- Only 38.3 percent of adults opened a Yellow Pages directory within the last year. (source: According to Experian Simmons 2010 *National Consumer Survey*).

I was shocked when I opened our local Yellow Pages because of the number of restaurants that had multiple page menus including prices. Why would a business owner throw away money by paying to put their menu in publication that the majority of people never use? Incidentally, many of these businesses did not list a website address, nor did they have a call to action (CTA). If the restaurant owners had asked people to register for coupons and specials in these ads, they could have at least started a conversation but instead the return on their considerable investment is likely very low.

Radio

MP3 players, internet radio and satellite radio directly impact the reach that local market radio has over certain target audiences. How many people younger than thirty go anywhere without their own personal listening devices that play the music they want to hear...

---

[14] http://sfgsa.org/Modules/ShowDocument.aspx?documentid=7555

uninterrupted? If I am listening to the radio, which is usually when I am alone in my car, I will change the channel or turn it off instead of having my thoughts interrupted with the babble of noise that advertisers are trying to get me to listen to. Pity the marketers who have identified me as a target market to get my attention with traditional radio ads. If you decide that radio ads work for your business, I suggest that you leverage the ad by having an immediate benefit if the listener does something either by as texting "a keyword" to "a phone number or mobile short code" or joining a VIP club by emailing "email address" to receive a special offer.

Guerrilla marketers know that there is one type of radio programming that is better for advertising – talk radio – because people are listening to opinion and educational material. If you can find a talk radio show that your ideal customer listens to for information that is relevant to your business, then create an ad that fits in with the show and be sure to include an immediate CTA.

Newspapers

Local newspapers are one of the traditional marketing sources that are not yet a complete write-off for my business. However, you really have to know your market and you need to test and track each and every ad to be sure that you are getting the best return on your investment. If you are not seeing results then try something else. I use my local twice-weekly newspaper for press releases which results in inquiries for my services. I also wrote a travel column which led to being hired by a college to facilitate a course on the "ABSeas of Cruising". However, each and every time I placed ads they failed to generate a return, so I no longer use display ads.

If you can establish yourself as the expert in your community for what your business offers by writing a column in the local paper, go for it! If you own a restaurant that sources ingredients primarily from your local market, you could write about your locally grown, seasonal ingredients, why they are healthy, what to look for when buying those products and provide a recipe. If you are a successful hotelier, you could write in the business section about marketing, cost savings, hiring, training and other areas of business that help local business owners, who may just choose your property to host an event, while recommending you to out-of-town visitors.   If you are a DMC, tour operator, destination marketing organization (DMO) or tour guide create a series of destination "insider information" articles that your ideal client would value and submit them to the newspapers that your prospects read.

You need to know your market though. When I wrote the travel column, resulting clients who contacted me and purchased from me were older and they were looking for a cruise or package vacation. At that time, they were my ideal target market. If you own a nightclub or restaurant that caters to the twenty-somethings, your audience does not read newspapers, so why bother? Instead go where your audience is, which is: mobile phones and social media.

Magazines

Magazines are kept longer and shared more often than newspapers and other printed material. However, lead times are long for magazine ads and it is often hard to determine the direct correlation between a magazine ad and a sale. However, if you are a niche tour operator or own a boutique hotel, magazines that your ideal customer reads may provide return on investment (ROI).

Certain magazines have a prestige value that can be worth more in the long term and can be leveraged for years. Guerrillas know that you can buy a full page ad in a national magazine's lowest priced region and use the ad again and again in future marketing campaigns (for example "As seen in *Time* magazine or *Condé Nast Traveler*").

If you can contribute an article to a magazine, you can benefit from the exposure to a targeted niche. I find that the smaller, industry specific magazines are much easier to work with than the more well-known publications.

Finally, if you can attract a writer to write about your destination or your tour in a travel or niche magazine and his or her experience is positive, the result could be far more valuable than paid advertising.

Television

TiVo, Netflix and internet TV are reducing the likelihood your television ad will be seen, so if you do choose to advertise on TV, pick your slots wisely and only advertise during programming that your ideal customer watches, to solve problems, get educated or be entertained. As with other advertising, be sure to have an appealing offer and a simple CTA that includes getting those prospects on an email, mobile and/or traditional mailing list. So, what shows, on what stations, at what times, does your ideal customer tune into?

Billboards

Look around you when you are in the vicinity of a billboard. Where are the eyes of the people who are around you? Where are the eyes of people you suspect to be your ideal customers? If they are looking at the billboards then this is an easy way to determine if a billboard will bring you exposure. However, if their eyes are glued to their phone your efforts will not produce results as your billboard will not be noticed.

Guerrilla Marketing Opportunities

There are some guerrilla marketing weapons that are particularly useful to tourism businesses. In this section, I concentrate on offline weapons and in later chapters I will explore digital marketing weapons.

Trade Shows

I attend many trade shows each year and I love seeing a great booth, with a great hook and fantastic representatives engaging with the visitors. Sadly though, there are many businesses that attend these trade shows without getting a return on investment. There are far too many boring booths, with people sitting behind a desk covered in brochures. The booth signage does not tell me what the business does, who their ideal customer is, what makes them unique and why I should stop and talk to them. Instead of "XYZ Tours" being the main message, change your message to get people imagining what you offer, for example:

"Experience the Beauty of Vancouver Island

The Thrill of Watching Grizzly Bears, Whales, Wolves and Eagles and

The Irresistible Luxury of Trip Advisor's #1 Wilderness Adventure"

You should have videos and beautiful photography to support your message, delivered by people that are engaging with the booth visitors using a give-away designed to capture names, emails and mobile phone numbers.

The return on the trade show investment will be substantially higher when you have a strong message for your ideal customer that differentiates both your business from your competitors and your booth from all the others on the trade show floor.

We had a promotion[15] for our incentive software booth at the Motivation Show in Chicago a few years ago that was featured in Successful Promotions Magazine. Poker was very popular at that time, so we created a campaign around a poker hand. We mailed out three cards of the same suit to our prospects, along with an invitation to stop at our booth to play a poker hand with us to win a prize (a deck of cards with our logo on them). Our tag line was "Don't Gamble with Your Incentive Software – Use Nexcentec's Incentive Suite". Our response rate of five percent was more than double what we expected and we achieved what we set out to do, which was to attract resellers.

One more suggestion that will save you money while saving the environment – forget about taking cases of brochures with you. Instead of piling them into the bags of the booth visitors, who are usually too polite to say no, put your brochures online. Turn your connection to your booth visitors into one where you ask questions that helps to qualify the visitor and then explain how they can get that exact information emailed to them immediately simply by texting "keyword" to a "short code" on their mobile phone (this is explained in the mobile marketing chapter). After they follow these instructions, they will receive an auto-responder text back to their phone with a link to download the document. When they go to download the document you can add another step to enter their name and email. This process gives you their name, email and mobile phone number and you have saved them the trouble of taking your brochures home with them, tossing them in the recycling at their hotel or, worse, waiting for you to get back to the office to send them the information they have requested. You have also saved yourself the cost of the brochure, the cost of shipping and you have been given three very important pieces of data to continue your conversation with them. If the person really wants a brochure you can satisfy them by setting up one of the keywords to respond with a request to complete the mailing address form. A coworker at your office can then mail the brochure the same day.

---

[15] http://www.asicentral.com/asp/open/news/successfulpromotions/janfeb/department5.asp

Networking and Conferences

If you attend networking events and conferences to build your prospect database, remember the golden rule to give before you ask. It is a complete turn-off to have sales people ask qualifying questions and then thrust their card in your face. Instead, approach networking events in a way where you ask the other person about themselves such as "How did you get to where you are today" and "How you can I help you become more successful? Let them talk about themselves and finish up by offering a solution. Granted, some people may be taken aback by such a "strange" approach and they may not share any ways in which you could help them but give it a try. You may end up with a new customer, friend and fantastic referrer to your business.

Window Displays / Lobby Displays

If your ideal customer does not constantly have their heads down while tapping away on their phone the entire time they are at your business, you may want to consider window displays and/or lobby displays. Just remember to make it relevant, with a CTA that starts or nurtures a relationship with them. Why not ask them to join your birthday club or VIP club by taking a specific action?

Testimonials, Reviews and Letters of Recommendation

Social proof is necessary to succeed and testimonials and reviews are no cost guerrilla marketing weapons with tremendous value to earn social proof. Ask your customers to write a testimonial or a review and then scan them and put them on your website and social media accounts. Also, ask your customers to post digital reviews to your website, to whatever digital review website is driving the most traffic to you.

Email List / Direct Mail List...With Opt-in Permission

Guerrilla marketers know that the relationship they have with their customer and prospect lists is more valuable than gold and they treat their lists with respect. They promise to only use the list for the reason that the person agrees to and they do not send spam or irrelevant emails. They also only send information after they have received permission to do so. Occasionally, the guerrilla marketer may add a fusion marketing offer, in the form of an endorsement and an exclusive offer to one of their regular mailings, but the guerrilla marketer would never jeopardize their relationship by sending offers for something that the customer did not agree to.

The way we market to our prospects and communicate with our customers will continue to evolve and savvy guerrillas will continue to test combinations of weapons to ensure their budgets produce the best returns.

Chapter 6 – Guerrilla Selling

"As you've noticed, people don't want to be sold. What people want is news and information about the things they care about".

Larry Weber

In this chapter you will read two very different guerrilla selling strategies. The first is good-old-fashioned-hit-the-pavement-gumption and the second is using personality-based marketing to tailor your message to close more sales.

Filling the Quality Inn, Orlando

I interviewed Harris Rosen, Founder and President of Rosen Hotels and Resorts, and he shared one of the most inspiring guerrilla selling stories that I have heard. Mr. Rosen used one-to-one marketing to fill his hotels, which was a low-cost way to build long lasting relationships.

> *"It was, as I recall, late 1973, or very early 1974, and there was an Arab oil embargo in effect. As you can imagine, this created a terrible problem for the Orlando tourism industry. The vast majority of hotels in Orlando were in very serious financial difficulty because travel was down approximately 70 percent. I thought perhaps this might be a great time for me to buy a hotel, because they were just about giving them away. I shopped and shopped for months and worked hard to put together a very detailed marketing plan. Finally I found a little Quality Inn hotel, right off Interstate 4 and on International Drive. I walked in, and asked to see the owner. Fortunately, the owner was in and came out of his office to greet me. He introduced himself to me as John Morgan and asked how he could be of assistance. I said that I was interested in buying a hotel, and this looked like the perfect one for me. Suddenly, he hugged me, and said that God had sent me to him.*
>
> *He shared with me how awful his life had become. He stated that business was so bad. He was hardly ever able to get home to see his wife and three daughters. We talked and he agreed to arrange a meeting between me, himself, and the hotel's lender (Travelers Insurance Company out of Connecticut). Several days later I met with a young man from Travelers. We*

talked for a while and he saw my resume and was really impressed. He said that based on my resume he thought that I would be a great owner-operator. He did ask me how much money I had in the bank; I was curious about the question and wondered what concern that was of his. I decided however to answer the question and I told him that I had $20,000 in the bank, and he said that was exactly what the down payment would be. I just knew that I had made a terrible mistake, but I decided to write a check for $20,000, and I agreed to assume the mortgage and prayed that I had made the right decision.

On June 24, 1974, I walked into "my" hotel and my office and I cried, because I believed that I had just really blown it and had made a terrible mistake. I quickly recovered and decided to put my marketing plan into effect. I asked a lady friend to stay at the hotel, and manage it for a few days while I went on my sales trip. She was a bit concerned, but I said, the hotel has 256 rooms, and rarely are more than 20 occupied, so do not worry about it. I did not have enough money to fly to New York so I hitchhiked. My plan was to visit the major motor coach operators in New York City, New Jersey and Massachusetts. I knew that buses were still coming to Orlando despite the oil embargo primarily because you could put 44 people on a bus, fill the bus with gas, and you were good to go. I visited with the owners of the major bus companies in each state who when they heard my story were really amazed that I had hitchhiked and expressed a real desire to help me.

They felt so badly for me, that they actually drove me to their competitors. I know it is crazy, but they did. They were all really wonderful and we still do business with many of them, even 38-years-later. I did bring with me little business cards that I had made, and I would give a card to each owner, and ask them to write a room rate on the card, stating that whatever rate they wrote on the card, that would be the rate I would charge them for the next year. They often asked, "What rate do you suggest?" and I would answer, "Whatever rate you want." That was in 1974, the rates they wrote down were anywhere from $7.25 a night to $8.25 a night. After they wrote their preferred rate, I told them that when I returned to

Orlando I would send a letter confirming the rates they had requested.

As it turned out Paragon Tours, a very large and successful motor-coach organization in New Bedford, Massachusetts was one of the last stops I made. Jim Penler, the owner, said that he knew of a couple that was driving to central Florida and they would be happy to take me back home so I would not have to hitchhike.

I left Massachusetts in style. The very nice couple drove me all the way back to Orlando. So appreciative was I for their kindness that they stayed with me as my guests for several months each year for the next 15 years until they both passed away.

It was not very long before motor coaches started coming to the Quality Inn, like crazy. No doubt, we were the busiest little motel in Orlando and yes, we were blessed even when just three months after we purchased the motel, the oil embargo was lifted. Soon lenders were visiting me on a fairly regular basis, asking me to please consider purchasing other hotels. One lender in particular was of interest to me. They had a hotel down the street, on International Drive, "The Solage" and they begged me to put an offer together. I did. It was a very attractive offer for me and a fair offer for them... Much to my surprise, they accepted and we closed on the hotel, exactly one year to the day after closing on the Quality Inn which of course was June 24, 1974. On June 24, 1975, I purchased my second hotel which I renamed the "International Inn" so in one year I went from owning nothing with $20K to my name in the bank to owning two hotels with a total of 500 rooms, and this was just the beginning."

Mr. Rosen had studied hotel management at Cornell and advanced management at the University of Virginia in Charlottesville, VA. He had worked for many years in a number of roles at the Waldorf-Astoria, Hilton, Disney and at an independent hotel in Acapulco before he bought his first hotel. Mr. Rosen has education, experience, skills and a marketing plan but, above all, he has a guerrilla's mindset. His vision, creativity, tenacity and relationships helped him grow his company to include seven properties in Orlando and he supports, among other projects, The Rosen School of Hospitality in Orlando... and it all started with a unique way to fill his hotels back in 1974.

Today, you can use one-to-one marketing to grow your own business – from providing customized products and services that individual customers appreciate, to fusion marketing arrangements (explored in a later chapter) and engaging with people in traditional and social networking environments you can increase your profits by leveraging your relationships – one person at a time.

Filling Your Beds and Seats using Personality-based marketing

I also had the pleasure of interviewing Jay Rosenberg, President of JSR Advertising Corporation, who is a social scientist and creator of The Quant Method® (TQM®), http://quantmethod.com. Here is an excerpt from the interview. The complete interview can be found at http://carolwain.com

> *"Over the course of my years at the agency we had some bumps. That is when I learned about personality marketing and that is how we recruited new clients in a very competitive industry when other agencies were having difficulties.*
>
> *There are four types of personalities: Diplomat, Mastermind, Thinker and Olympian. We could speed read the personality types on the telephone with prospects. When they came for an office tour, we knew that the Diplomats would like to meet lots of people. Diplomats love people. Masterminds just want to have a business meeting. They do not need to meet people. Masterminds are very objective types. Diplomats are quite subjective; they are very 'feeling' people. We got to a level where we knew what kind of tour to give them. What they would like for lunch. We knew pretty much how they would dress and we knew all kinds of things.*
>
> *That really worked well one-on-one and I always thought if I could do only this on a mass basis. I teamed up with a firm that goes all the way back to Myers-Briggs®, their founder. We created a two minute test. With that two minute test, we can determine the personality types of the people who take it. From that, we have sales tactics, our sales psychology that we guide our clients with so that they can be more effective and influence their prospects and clients.*

Olympians are very responsive to shiny objects. They do not like facts, but they love to talk about themselves and they love testimonials and stories. They love incentives which would be great for employees or for guests that are coming, little extras. I think a lot of people who are Olympians would be interested and very responsive to tourism on the consumer side because they are very sense-driven. They like new things, they like to explore. They like fun, glamorous, exciting, adventurous things to do. Olympians would be one of the personality types that would be very nice to reach and to address in this kind of selling.

Famous Olympians included Marlon Brando as the Godfather. Elvis Presley, Donald Trump, the Cowardly Lion from the Wizard of Oz. The Olympians do not like the details, but the Thinker loves details. They adore details. No detail is too small. If I were a hotel and I knew that my prospect was a Thinker, I would give them a very organized, step-by-step presentation about the hotel and the amenities. We also know they do not like risk. They like everything to be logical and thorough. Of the four personality types, they are the last one to make a decision to buy. You want to start months before because they decide to buy after they analyze all the details. If they go with you, they become very good customers because once they commit, they really commit. They are very good candidates for back-end offers because they always want more details. Upsell Thinkers because if you offer them extra things to buy it will really increase your bottom line.

More than half of the Presidents of the United States were Thinkers. Warren Buffet, the investor, is a Thinker and so is the Queen of England. Donald Duck is also a Thinker.

The Thinker is a complete opposite from the Olympian who is just out for fun and sensual adventure in terms of the five senses. The Thinker is the one that we will call the 'corporate suit type.'

When it comes to Diplomats, Diplomats are family-driven and people-driven. They are very feeling, as I said before. They'd be great for families. They are fabulous for referrals. Of the four types, the Diplomat is the one that is going to be the best connector. They love to connect. Martin Luther King was a Diplomat and he sure connected. Diplomats love guidance in everything they do. When they meet you, they bestow their friendship on you. You must never cross them because Diplomats do not like conflict and they hate to say no. Even if you do cross them they will say yes but they will not remain your friend. You have got to be warm and supportive and encouraging in selling to them. More than any other personality type, they love a big guarantee. They want almost your personal guarantee to minimize their risk. They are conservative. They want to like you, before they want to do business with you. Use a soft sale technique because they do not want to be put on the spot. They are very often supportive of causes like PETA. Diplomats can sometimes go to sleep at night, thinking about how they are going to help someone. They use the word 'actualizing' themselves because they think there is a higher destiny and by helping others they get there. Oprah Winfrey, Martin Luther King, Regis Philbin and Princess Diana are Diplomats. (So is Carol Wain.)

The fourth person, the fourth type is the Mastermind. The Mastermind is a little bit out there. They are imagination-type people. Steve Jobs, Einstein, Bill Gates, Thomas Edison are Masterminds, as are a lot of engineers. They are distracted with all this thinking going on in their head and they can seem to be out there and not friendly. They do not mind an aggressive sales approach. A Diplomat does not like aggression, nor does the Thinker, but a Mastermind does not mind it at all. It shows them that the salesperson knows what they are talking about. They do not like a long presentation because they value their time highly and if you were going to pitch them, you would say, 'This will save you time. It will give you more time for your more important things.' Time is very important to them. They are driven by efficiency, competence, logic and reason. They are not bashful about overruling their boss and listening to subordinates' ideas. They are open to everybody's ideas and they like to take all these ideas and come up with their own result. If you do not offer an itinerary to a Mastermind, give him options and let him decide what his trip is going to be like. There is an expression, 'If the facts do not comport to my thinking, so much for the facts.' That is what a Mastermind would say.

Masterminds are 14 percent, Thinkers are 46 percent, Diplomats are 17 percent and Olympians are 23 percent of the population. That is in the whole world. People travel to little villages in New Guinea and to Tokyo and to New York City and all over the world. There are only these four types. There are four subtypes to each one but everybody's eyes would glaze over if we talked about them."

I then asked Jay how a hotel, a DMC or someone who is selling to meeting planners would they go about defining their type and selling strategy. He responded:

"You can do it on the phone by conversation and of course if you are doing it with the test, it would be real easy. On a phone call, the Masterminds and the Olympians are more assertive. They will say, 'Tell me about this trip?' The Thinker and the Diplomats are more reserved. They would say, 'Would you tell me about this trip' in a softer voice. A Thinker, who is this detailed person, when you give them a number they would say that is, '$1,593 and that includes...' there are little tips, there is guidance. Of course, doing it yourself on the phone is not going to be 100 percent, but you get there. There are about maybe six or seven ways to do it, but people give away their personality types just in the conversation. If you have the same personality type as they happen to have, that is great because you will get along wonderfully except for the Masterminds, who are very competitive.

That is the way to do it on a one-to-one level on the phone. In person, is a plus because, for example, the Olympian lives big. They are going to have big hoop earrings. The women will have bigger jewelry; they will be coming up in a more dramatic vehicle. The guys will say, "Let us go to your club for lunch." Where the Thinkers would never be like that. They are more corporate-looking; they are dressed up in conservative clothes. So visually you can tell as well. Once you get your brain around how the test works, you can interpret the ones you do not have the test for.

On a mass scale, you have got four personality types and you are selling a trip to Paris and a hotel. You have got four messages and each one would be slightly tuned to cover the details, if it is a Thinker; and talk about the fun and have testimonial if it is an Olympian; and tone it also for the other two. About a year ago, I worked with an Irish tour operator and they got a big kick out of this thinking, they thought it was really good.'

I then asked "For the mass market, how would you know which way to market to that person when you really do not know that person?" Jay responded "You ask him questions. What is the most important thing you would like to see? What are your most burning questions about your forthcoming trip to London? You ask more questions. You find out what they want. People appreciate these questions because it means that we are caring. We are thinking about helping them and their best interests."

It is also introduces this 'cognitive overload'. Google released an article called The Zero Moment of Truth[16]. *Everybody seems to be shopping online before they go to a store. People go to the baby food website and read the ingredients rather than stand in the store and read them. When you know this, if you can create communications that have a laser-sharp focus on what they want to know, you do not give them this overload that they do not want. People have taken this overload and they have had a melt-down and they do the simplicity thinking, 'I will just try something.' There was a recent study and they said, 'The marketing funnel has gone to a marketing tunnel.' People do not want to take this traditional path to purchase. They just want something that works and works well for them. That is why a lot of people buy the Apple iPhone – because you do not have to do a lot of homework – you know it is going to be a good product.*
Customarily, when we create a marketing campaign, we develop what we call a control piece. You have a magazine offer or product offer and you spend hours and weeks and

---

16 http://www.zeromomentoftruth.com/

years developing this really laser sharp offer. We have found that people need to create four controls, one for each personality type. You will have your fundamental control, but you will have to tune it because if you give an Olympian all sorts of details, you will lose them. If you talk to a Thinker with kind of a slap on the back, laugh-out-loud manner of the Olympian you are going to scare off the Thinker. Each personality type needs their own little set of marketing pieces, which do not have to be too different but they have to be sensitive to the variables within the personality type."

Which personality type are you? If you need more help, you can take the two minute quiz on the TQM website and you can contact Jay at jay@quantmethod.com.

As clients begin to trust and like you they will find more value in their relationship with you and will have a better user experience. Best of all, they are much more inclined to buy from you, which is a win-win situation.

These are two very unique ways to increase your sales. Which suits your business and personality more? What creative ways can you devise to fill your seats or beds?

Chapter 7 – Digital Public Relations and Online Review Management

"It takes many good deeds to build a good reputation, and only one bad one to lose it"

Benjamin Franklin

For many business owners, one of the biggest hurdles to leaping onto the internet is realizing that people will be talking about your company whether you like it or not. Mistakes are bound to happen in any business, but when they do it is quite possible that the story will wind up on the internet – forever – where anyone searching for your business can find it.

There are two components to managing your online reputation: Digital Public Relations (PR) and Online Review Management. Digital PR refers to how you communicate with people who are talking about your business in a review website or on social media. Online review management has a reactive component – Digital PR – and it has a proactive component – actively soliciting online feedback from happy customers.

These statistics show how important Digital PR and managing your online reputation is:

- "51% of hotel guests state that 'guest experience factors' which include past experience, reputation, recommendations, and online reviews, are critical to selecting a hotel. This factor is more important to guests than hotel location (48%) and price (42%)." (source: Market Metrix, January 2010).
- "Travelers spend an enormous amount of time researching hotels online. On average, hotel consumers made 12 visits to an OTA's website, requested 7.5 pages per visit, and spent almost 5 minutes on each page before booking." (source: Cornell University research, April 2011).
- A negative review or comment on the Twitter, Facebook or YouTube websites can result in a loss of approximately 30 customers (source: Convergys Corp).
- 75% of people do not believe that companies tell the truth in advertisements. (source: Yankelovich).
- 90% of consumers online trust recommendations from people

they know; 70% trust opinions of unknown users. (source: Econsultancy, July 2009).

Guerrillas know that if you are not maintaining an effective presence on the web and managing your Digital PR, you may have two problems:

- You will not have a chance to explain the situation and fix it so you can respond to customer issues in a mutually acceptable manner; and
- The negative review could wind up ranking high in the search results, so whenever somebody searches for your business, this could be one of the first things they see. The review might be accurate if a mistake really was made, or it might be completely inaccurate, but that potential customer has no way of knowing for sure and they will likely take the review at face value.

The solution is to be a part of the conversation. In other words, engage your customers on the sites where these kinds of reviews may appear so you can try to correct any mistakes that were actually made, explain your side if it is completely inaccurate and thank your customers for posting about their positive experience.

It is also important to have an active presence on Facebook, Twitter, LinkedIn, TripAdvisor, Urban Spoon, Google, Yelp and Pinterest as a point of contact for your customers who are already in those places.

Consider This

One of your employees has been dealing with a customer, and the customer is unhappy with the service he received. Instead of coming to you and giving you the opportunity to fix the problem, he goes to a review website and posts about the problem and how unhappy he was with your company. If you do not have a presence there, you might never know about it. Yet people who are looking for information about your company online will quite likely find that information whenever they search for you.

If you are active on those sites, you can jump in and try to correct the situation. This is not only going to give you a chance to turn an unhappy customer into a happy one (who might also become one of your biggest supporters at that point) but it is also going to add your side of things to the "record" of the situation on the internet. Now when someone searching for you finds that review/complaint, they are also going to see your response, and that you tried to rectify the situation for that unhappy customer.

Guerrilla Tip: Knowing what is being said about you is the first line of defense and there are social media monitoring services, such as Trackur[17], Social Mention[18], Netvibes[19] or Topsy[20] that will track mentions of your business online so that you can see what is being written. You should also set up a Google Alert (http://google.com/alerts) for your business name but I would not recommend relying solely on that service as it is not as thorough as a social monitoring service.

Here are some of today's more popular websites that include a review component:

- Yelp.com
- Google Plus (https://plus.google.com)
- Where.com
- Citysearch.com
- Zagat.com
- Yahoo Local (http://local.yahoo.com)
- Google Maps (https://maps.google.com)
- UrbanSpoon.com
- TripAdvisor.com
- Hotels.com
- Expedia.com
- Hotwire.com

There may also be regional review websites or industry-specific review websites that could be more useful to your business so search for the most popular websites that your customers use.

One of the reasons these sites are so important is many of them have apps for the iPhone and other smart phones and many people use them to look up local businesses when they are on the go. If they find a listing with low ratings or bad reviews, they can choose a competitor

---

[17] http://trackur.com
[18] http://socialmention.com
[19] http://netvibes.com
[20] http://topsy.com

and the business owner will never know if she lost a potential customer.

An Interview with Andreas Schmidt

I spoke with Andreas Schmidt, the General Manager for the number one TripAdvisor hotel in Cancun, Le Blanc Spa Resort, about the value of TripAdvisor to their business. During our interview (which can be found at http://carolwain.com) he said:

> *"Our service is a personalized service. We really try to care about our customers and the service should not end when the guests are leaving the resort. We should still maintain a relationship with them. We should be thankful for any feedback they are they giving us. If it is good then it is motivational for the staff. If it is not so good it is an opportunity for us to improve.*
>
> *So, in the past, really, if you went to TripAdvisor or other review sites, you would never find any comments or responses to the guests. But, when a guest sits down for an hour or two hours writing a review, it really deserves some response because it is still a service. If you ask for something at the resort, our responsibility is to make it happen for you and if we cannot make it happen at least you expect an answer. It is the same thing with all social media. You expect and you deserve an answer and we (at the resort) should be thankful for any response we are getting and you should be noted.*
>
> *So basically, we started 2½ years ago and it became really huge. TripAdvisor, and unfortunately I cannot put it down in numbers, is probably the most important sales engine for us now. Everybody is doing it, I do it, and you do it too. You make a reservation, you look at the hotel, you look for rates, you compare hotels and before you make your final decision you will go to TripAdvisor... at least 80 percent of the guests do.*
>
> *And then it comes back to the little details which make a difference. You get welcomed here with a cold towel, and a flower and coconut water. When you check TripAdvisor you see that there are comments and the General Manager is answering the comments and you say 'Wow, the General*

Manager is answering the comments'. If you check with the competition, maybe, the Public Relations Manager is handling the comments, which is a nice touch. But then you think, 'they really do not care that much. The General Manager over there does it personally.' It is the little details.

It is really important to answer all of them because as you said, 'He did not answer mine'. So we did not fulfill all of your expectations which is a little cross that they are doing a great job but they are not perfect, so we still have opportunity to improve.

I talk on a daily basis to our guests and it will not happen ... ever... that I do not meet two or three or four guests a day who tell me that they chose the resort because of the reviews, so it is important to handle it in the right way.

My advice is if you are doing a great service, if you care about your customers you will do it. People in the hospitality business always talk about 'what is quality?' And then they talk about 'exceeding the expectations of the customers'... which is all nice and I agree but quality, in my opinion, is to get the 'wow' out of our customers and I want to get the wow out even after the guests are gone. I want to call you and have the butler call you when you get home to make sure that you got home all right. You are going to say 'wow'.

With TripAdvisor if you get an answer right away you want to say 'They even care even though I am not here anymore.' My advice is do not stop caring after they are gone."

Mr. Schmidt stated it well, it is all about caring and delighting customers and it is no wonder why the property is so well rated on TripAdvisor.

Negative Reviews

The impact of negative reviews can be devastating to a business. If people see one negative review and fifty positive reviews they are more likely to dismiss the negative review as being unrealistic. However, if people see one negative review, two neutral reviews and one glowing review, they may choose to try another less "risky" business. You cannot remove a negative review on most review websites and you should respond to them as part of your Digital PR strategy. Since negative reviews remain online forever, the best practice is to "bury" negative reviews with positive ones so negative reviews represent an anomaly.

Reality or Fantasy?

Before I explain how to bury a negative review, I'd like you to ask yourself, "Is my marketing consistent with reality?" because this is the easiest way to manage expectations. If you say that you are a five-star resort then you better be perfect in every way. There are too many businesses that claim to be what they are not. It is those businesses that are getting slammed by complaints because they are setting an expectation for an experience they cannot deliver. If your menu or point-of-purchase displays show photos of mouth-watering dishes, they better look like that when your customer buys them. If your business uses images that represent your business on opening day and it no longer looks that way, either change your images or invest in a refurbishment. Do not attempt to deceive people.

People are always enthusiastic when their expectations are exceeded, so if you have a three-star property, market yourself as a three-star property and then train your staff to over-deliver on the experience. It is also much easier (and less expensive) to hire well, treat your employees well and show them how to impress customers than it is to change the physical aspects of your business or its location.

Impressing the Hard-to-Please

Most people will remember the helpfulness and friendliness of the employees a lot longer than a stain on the carpet or an improperly cooked steak, so always deliver exceptional experiences. In my role as the owner of an incentive company that sells incentive travel, I stay at four and five-star properties and I am tuned-in to details most guests ignore. I look for everything which would detract from the guest experience and I note it. (Being a secret shopper was my favorite activity as a McDonald's manager.) I still remember a hotel sales manager's comment to me "Oh, you are one of those high-maintenance guests" and I suppose I am. I can point out every touch point which was exceptional, expected and needs improvement and if you would like me to secret shop your business, let me know.

As I was planning my trip to visit Jay and Jeannie Levinson in Debary, FL this year, I realized – gasp – there were no properties that were "incentive quality". I chose the Hampton Inn because it had the best reviews and I was glad I did. From the moment I walked through the door until the time I left, the genuine and friendly service blew me away. I arrived late and hungry and when I asked the front desk clerk where I could find some food, she gave me recommendations. When I came back a short while later (the restaurant she recommended had just closed) she was concerned and asked if I would like her to bake me some cookies. On another occasion, when I was in need of a bottle opener, a different front desk clerk removed hers from her keychain and gave it to me. When I asked to change rooms because of the highway noise, I was given a room with two queen beds, instead of a king bed which I had reserved. One of the housekeeping staff actually ran down the hall as I was moving rooms to tell me about the difference in beds and to ask if I was okay with the change (I was). The property is a three-star property because of the location, décor, facilities and amenities but the service was five-star all the way. Not only am I writing a fantastic review of the property in this book, I have also written about it on my blog and on TripAdvisor. This team certainly delivered service far exceeding my three-star expectations.

Burying Negative Reviews

If your marketing represents reality and your employees are delivering on your brand promise, the best way to bury negative reviews and to benefit from having positive reviews is to actively request reviews, testimonials and ratings from your customers. Here are some ideas:

- Use an "old-fashioned" customer comment card;
- Generate a Quick Response (QR) code that lands on your listing on the sites that brings you the most business. That could be Yelp, or TripAdvisor, or Zagat, or Google;
- Create an email survey shortly after customers have purchased from you;
- Send a text message survey;
- Ask customers to videotape themselves enjoying what you are selling and send it to you so that you can post on your website and social media accounts;
- Find customers who are enjoying themselves and ask if they agree to be interviewed for your website;
- Ask customers to write about their experience on Facebook; and

- Ask happy customers for a letter of reference and / or a recommendation in LinkedIn.

If you have customers that fill in traditional guest comment cards, ask if they would permit you to use their comments online. When they agree (check with your lawyer to be sure you have the proper type of agreement) then scan their comment cards and upload the image along with a "description" that restates their review and post it to your website and on your social media accounts. When you describe the compliment in addition to scanning the image, you have "proof" of the review while the words become searchable online.

If you have hard copy reviews you choose which reviews to upload and I recommend uploading all positive reviews. However, do not fall into the trap of solely uploading positive reviews because your customers and potential customers will see through this strategy and it will backfire on you. After all, if all manually-added reviews are positive and the customer-added reviews are not, your attempt to deceive becomes obvious.

Instead add neutral reviews and even a review that might be both positive and negative so that your customers and potential customers see that your business is real. (Do not upload any bad reviews though, instead handle those offline.)

Warning: Do not launch a review campaign for short-term results because it is obvious the activity is abnormal. Instead start slowly, particularly if the reviews you currently have were posted sporadically. After you start, make it an ongoing process to request feedback through online reviews and comment cards and then follow-up with appropriate Digital PR.

Digital PR Disaster

There are many social media missteps that will affect brand image. Some examples include: telling "fans" not to post on your Facebook timeline, one-way communication and having a public argument on the timeline. The following example shows you just how much damage one brand can suffer, while another can capitalize.

This is the story of Mr. Thomas Cook, a 26 year old who posted on The Thomas Cook UK website in what appears to be a somewhat tongue-in-cheek manner. Instead of the Social Media Manager using humor to respond in kind, she responded in a business tone that ended up back-firing for Thomas Cook UK, while a competitor capitalized on the opportunity. Below are screen shots taken by Mr. Thomas Cook and posted to http://imgur.com/a/Lyo8S

Thomas Cook ▸ Thomas Cook UK

Hi Thomas Cook. Seeing as I share the exact same name as your huge company, and because of this I have been ridiculed since I can remember. I think it's only fair that you help compensate for this by giving me one of your lovely holidays. A weekend to Paris would do just fine. Thank you

Like · Comment · 15 November at 19.56 ·

Beth Elkington, Ruby MayNot Cook, Becca Dainty and 45 others like this.

Ewan Malone Go for it Thomas cook
15 November at 22:02 · Like

Ben Montgomery I study PR at university and I think this would be a fantastic PR opportunity. They would be fools not to do this.
16 November at 01:49 · Unlike · 1

Thomas Cook UK Hi Thomas
Great to hear from you! Unfortunately we are unable to give away free holidays. Please see www.thomascook.com for the best available prices. Have a nice weekend.
Lara

Thomas Cook | Cheap holidays, Package Holidays, Hotels, Flights
www.thomascook.com
Thomas Cook Holidays – £100 off October package holidays and up to £150 off Summer 2012 holidays. Don't just book it, Thomas Cook it.

16 November at 10:46 · Like

Thomas Cook Oh Thomas Cook, you have misunderstood me. I wasn't asking for a free holiday. I was asking for a holiday to compensate for the years of ridicule and tourment I have had to endure as a result of sharing your name, and also for helping to promote your brand by constantly keeping it in peoples minds every time they speak to me. Now I don't know what you pay your marketing team, but for 26 years of work I'd estimate that you owe me around £338,000 in salaries, so I think accepting a weekend to Paris as payment is very generous of me. You are welcome.
16 November at 16:24 · Like · 17

Charlotte Hunt of LowCostHolidays.com became aware of the post and, from her personal Facebook account she sent a personal message to Mr. Thomas Cook.

Charlotte Hunt

Dear Thomas Cook,
Lowcostholidays.com here, how are you today? We've seen that
you have recently made a request to the travel company Thomas
Cook UK to be compensated for the years of ridicule that you
have suffered for sharing their name. Here at
lowcostholidays.com we completely sympathise with your
suffering and if your name was 'lowcostholidays.com' we would
certainly have accepted your request to be sent away on a
weekend to Paris. So in Thomas Cook's time of crisis we thought
it was about time we stepped in to offer a helping hand to
customers like yourself who have found themselves, as we like to
say 'Thomas Crooked'. So how about we send you on that
weekend to Paris, in fact - why not make it a week for you and a
friend! What do you say?
Kind Regards
The Marketing team at lowcostholidays.com
https://www.facebook.com/lowcostholidays.com

lowcostholidays.com

Smiley and the team's mission is to try and bring a smile to all our fan's
faces with great competitions (we love giving away holidays), the best
holiday deals, and by getting our fans involved with a bit of fun and
games on Facebook. We want all of our customers to have confidence in
travelling with lowcostholidays.com so we have explained how being
protected by ABTA and ATOL means that we are a reliable holiday
company here - > http://www.lowcostholidays.com/holiday-
protection.htm
Page · 16,792 like this

Eleven months later, Mr. Thomas Cook and his friend took the offered trip and he posted photos about it online. The post quickly gained attention and it was the number one story on Reddit.com[21]. This story received attention on Twitter, with nearly 1,600 tweets two days after he posted his images to Imgur. LowCostHolidays.com received priceless publicity while Thomas Cook UK took a beating from people on Facebook, even after posting this attempt to smooth things over:

---

[21]
http://www.reddit.com/r/funny/comments/11mlvv/benifits_of_sharing_my_name_with_a_travel_
agent/

Just a quick one from the TC team to say we're genuinely pleased our namesake Thomas Cook looks like he's had a great time in Paris courtesy of LowCostHolidays.co.uk! http://tinyurl.com/ri1yoR5#ihPdq

Whilst we admire Mr Cook's plucky approach, we value all of our customers equally so we don't give free holidays to all of the Thomas or Thomasina Cooks who email us! (or even our colleagues who are called Thomas Cook too!)

But we do have a cause that WE believe is truly worthwhile which we've extended an invitation to Mr Cook to join us with. For the 10th year running we'll be taking hundreds of sick and disadvantaged children on a 'Flight of Dreams' to meet Father Christmas on board our own planes, and we wondered whether he'd like to join us and be part of the Thomas Cook volunteer team! Find out more at www.thomascookchildrenscharity.com

Furthermore, if you happen to be one the world's Thomas (or Thomasina!) Cooks – write to us with your birthday and wait and see what happens next...

Unfortunately, the post did not work as they hoped as people commented that their damage control was just as misguided as their original response.

Remember, what happens online stay online forever, so think about the long term impact of the decisions you make when engaging with people. Thomas Cook UK deleted the original post from their Facebook Page but as you see here, Mr. Thomas Cook took a screenshot which he posted in another website beyond the reaches of the brand. While it appears that Thomas Cook UK has decided to give a birthday gift to every Thomas or Thomasina Cook who writes to them, it would have been much more effective to have taken that stance a year ago. If I was their Social Media Manager, I would respond to the post in a similar tone and I would thank Mr. Thomas Cook for his post. I would say something along the lines of "You have given us a great idea, thank you Thomas Cook. As a result of your suggestion, we have created a sweepstakes and we invite all the Thomas and Thomasina Cooks in the UK to enter to win a weekend in Paris. Click here for details and to enter."

Take your Digital PR seriously or suffer the consequences.

Part Two –
Multi-Channel Marketing

In this section we explore ways to use multiple marketing channels to increase profitable sales and to engage your customers and prospects.

Multi-Channel Marketing Overview

Your ideal tourism customers are reading reviews, comparing rates, checking menus, looking at photos, sharing stories, looking for answers and making recommendations on tablets, smart phones, laptops and desktop computers. Your ideal customers may also be watching TV, listening to the radio and opening direct mail. Your job is to figure out how they are absorbing information and what offers they will find appealing using a variety of channels.

In my interview with James Schramko of SuperFastBusiness.com (available at http://carolwain.com) I asked him how he built such a successful business. James responded:

> *"The thing is you just have to have people find out about what it is that you do. You want multiple traffic pillars, as Jay Abraham would teach — the 'Parthenon Theory'. Imagine pipelines running into your business and you want lots of pipelines running in from different places. You identify 'What are the marketing channels through which you can easily access your perfect customer?' Then you start to learn about those traffic channels and identify how they work and who can teach you about accessing them or who can you pay to get a result from those traffic channels.*
>
> *Most people are aware of the standard ones like taking out an advertisement in the newspaper or sending fliers to people's homes. The traditional media channels are well-worn, but there are lots of new media channels that people are switching on to such as Facebook and having your own website and letting people find out about that website because of the good information you are putting there. We have this phenomenon of people being able to share good information.*
>
> *Now it is so easy for someone to click a "Like" button or a "Plus" button on a website and that immediately pops out in front of all of their friends. The idea starts with having something worth finding, having a product or a service that is good enough that people want to talk about it even if they are not paid to do it.*
>
> *The second side of it is actually paying for traffic or buying marketing visits through the various marketing channels that*

you feel are the most suited to your business. You might have a theory about what is best, but what you should do is test different ones and see what results you get.

Get comfortable with a few different traffic channels and then maximize those. I have found the ones that suit my business. You will see that I do a lot of videos and I do a lot of audio in my business because I know that firstly, most of my competitors are either too scared to go on camera or do not realize how valuable the audio channels are yet.

Secondly, people love to consume audios and videos. The average American is watching 6 hours of video every day and they are multitasking. They are watching television with an iPad on their lap. They are also all plugged into smart phones and iPads with iTunes. When you start doing things like podcasts you get to be with people while they are jogging or catching a bus to work. You can be places where people can access video and may not be reading."

Chapter 8 – Internet Marketing

"Authenticity, honesty, and personal voice underlie much of what is successful on the Web"

Rick Levine

Internet Marketing Overview

The topic of internet marketing is huge and could easily fill a book or two, so for our Guerrilla Tourism Marketing purposes I will cover four components of internet marketing:

- Keywords;
- Website;
- Email Marketing; and
- Search Engine Marketing;

In the chapter that helped you to define your ideal customer, you learned how to get inside her head so that you could speak to her in ways that she would relate to. In the Guerrilla Selling chapter, you learned how the various personality types like to communicate and process information that helps them to make a purchase. Let us explore how you can use keywords and your website to catch the attention of your ideal customer.

Keywords

Understanding keywords is important for everything related to internet marketing, from the words you use in your business descriptions, to your press releases, website copy, articles, images, blog posts, blog tags, blog categories, comments and so much more. Keywords are used for search engine optimization (SEO), search engine marketing (SEM) and to attract your ideal customer. It is a concept that can be a little intimidating but guerrilla marketers know that guesswork is not in our toolbox, so take the time to choose your keywords wisely.

Keywords are the words that people use when looking for exactly what you offer. People are becoming more sophisticated in their searches as they know that one-word or two-word keyword phrases will not give them what they are looking for, except perhaps a page from Wikipedia. Instead, they make their searches more complex, a

"Long Tail Keyword Phrase", which is great for you and great for the search engine user – your potential customer.

Instead of typing "Holiday Florida" or "Vacation Florida", savvy search engine users will type a phrase that suits what they are really looking for such as "Honeymoon Key West romantic small resort." The difference between the simple search and the long tail keyword phrase search is enormous. These users know where they want to go and what size resort they are looking for to enjoy their honeymoon. They are quite far along in their research because they have already eliminated many destinations and types of accommodation. If your ideal customer includes honeymooners and you have a small resort in Key West then you have a match that will be much easier to turn into a sale.

In the Guerrilla Marketing Workbook, which can be purchased on my website at http://carolwain.com you will find more detail about how to find suitable keywords for your business. For the purposes of this book, I suggest you use the Google Keyword Tool (https://adwords.google.com) to see what the most popular keyword phrases are for your type of business. The help section there is useful to guide you through the process. The search for "honeymoon Key West romantic small resort" produced zero results in both the "Exact Match" and "Broad Search", which means that either no-one or very few people have typed this exact phrase. That is okay because Google presents suggestions for other terms that have been searched. Go through the list and look at the search terms that would match your business. The more specific you can be the better because you want the right people to visit your website and either buy, or respond to your Call to Action (CTA).

In the results you will notice that there is a column for "competition". If you see a "high" competition, this means that people are competing for this specific phrase in Google AdWords. Unless you have a huge budget for AdWords, I would caution you to find a more suitable term with less competition... a term that your ideal customer would use to find exactly what you are offering.

Another interesting component of this keyword tool is when you find a phrase that looks good, click on it and then click on the Google Insights option. This shows you the trends for that phrase and other similar terms.

You can also type your keyword phrases into the Google search to see what results are presented. Make note of the top 10 results. Are any of them your competitors? Once you have compiled your list of specific keyword phrases, you will use them over and over again, as you are creating your websites and writing descriptions for your images.

Your Website

I asked James Schramko, SuperFastBusiness.com, what the most common mistakes are on websites. His response was:

>*"A lot of people still do this selfish marketing. You go to their home page and it says, 'Welcome to my Web page.' 'I do this, I do that, we do this; we do that.' It is all about them and not the customer, so that is a very common mistake. They have not really thought through what action they would like people to take when they come to their website. Sometimes they will be serving up a buffet of a thousand things and the customer is paralyzed and cannot make any decision at all. They've got some obscure video there that has no CTA – that does not tell people what to do – and people do not even know what it is when they look at it. I have seen those extremes.*

>*The best thing they could do is to have a very simple, clear offer and make it obvious what they would like people to do when they come to their website. What sort of action would they like people to take? I think it is tempting in the tourism industry because there are so many variables, but the most successful companies have very few options. If you want an example of that, go to Google.com and you will see this one box on the page and search bar. There is almost nothing on the page and it is obvious that people were to type something in and go for it. That has become a wildly successful website.*

>*It is identifying their perfect customer and making sure their perfect customer knows that they exist.*

>*One thing is make it very simple and easy to navigate because that helps the person visiting your website find that they would to find. 'Less is more' is a good maxim there. Secondly, be very clear about the CTA that you would like people to take. For most businesses it would be a good idea to put their*

telephone number on the top right hand side of the website because if they have a telephone service or they are able to receive telephone calls a lot of people going to their website are simply looking for the phone number to contact these people. If you do not put it on the top right hand side of the website you are going against convention and now you make it really hard for people to contact you.

The other actions that you might want people to take are to either join up for some kind of newsletter or training sequence or you may want to go directly for a sale or purchase transaction. Whatever you do, make sure that anything you think is important appears above the fold, which means that the customer does not have to scroll to find it. As soon as you have to scroll you lose most of your viewers, they drop off dramatically as soon as you have to scroll. Anything you want to happen should be easily visible on an average computer without scrolling."

Your website marketability and profitability is based on how well it is able to convert your visitors to paying customers and considering you only have about three seconds to make an impression, it is critical that you do this properly. Here are some essentials that will turn your website into a profit producing machine:

Professional, Clean Layout

Your website should be clean, professional and easy to navigate if you want visitors to stick around for any amount of time. Confusing websites only cause visitors to hit the back button as they search for information or products. Do not make people wait for your content to load. Many businesses make the mistake of overcrowding their websites with stuff that their visitors really do not care about. Your website, especially your home page, should be built to grab attention quickly so people can find what they are looking for, including contact info and a CTA.

Lead Capture

If you have not already heard this before, you will hear it often from guerrilla marketers, "The money is in the relationship with your list". Building a list of customers and leads should be the priority of any business owner and your website is a great place to collect that contact information. One of the easiest ways to capture leads is by installing a lead capture system on your website. This can be a form that asks visitors to enter their name and email address in exchange for something they will value. You could use a contest or sweepstakes or a "share with a friend" promotion. When you know your ideal customer, you will know what they value. Once you have these leads in your sales funnel, you can then start sending emails to them about your company. The primary focus should be about building a relationship with the people on your list and you should only send relevant promotions from time to time. When done correctly, you will build loyalty. Keep sending them relevant content related to the information requested when they signed up.

Strong Call to Action

Every page on your website should have a CTA. Some businesses want their prospects to call them, some want them to email them, and some want them to come into their establishment. Your CTA will be determined when you create your marketing plan. CTAs have proven to help businesses convert more website visitors into actual, paying customers. Some people simply need to be told what to do when they reach your website, so ask them to take a specific action and they often will.

Do not just say "Call Us Today." Instead, say, "Call Us Today at 877-206-9950". If you want them to come into your establishment, do not just say "Come See Us Today." Instead, say, "Come See Us Today at XXX Main Street, City, and State." If you want your website visitors to sign-up for last minute deals using their mobile phone, tell them to text "a keyword" to "a phone number or short code" (this is explained in the Mobile Marketing Chapter).

Contact Us

Some business owners make the mistake of only putting their contact information on their "Contact Us" page. However, your phone number should be on all pages of your website to make it easy for your customers and prospects to get in touch with you. This is particularly important for people who find you using their mobile device as they will likely "tap to call" if they want to reach you by phone right away.

Also be sure to put a contact form on your Contact Us page so visitors can reach you from your website. This will give your visitors a variety of options when it comes to contacting you.

Features specific to travel websites

The "Show me the Money" features that people are looking for in a travel website.

Feature	2012
Being able to check lowest fares/rates	84%
Lowest price/rate guarantee	81
Photos of rooms/facilities	81
Easy to use booking feature	78
Ability to compare fares and rates	77
Scheduling activities in advance	70
Destination interactive maps	65
Ability to download coupons for savings	62
Email notification of specials	56
User generated reviews	56
Ability to share photo with others	30

[22]

Relevant Website Content

Content is king because people want be able to research for solutions to their problems on their own terms and on the devices they choose for their search. Users want to find information easily and search engines are constantly changing their algorithms so that quality content is presented as a result of a search. Users do not want to be bothered with pop-ups, ads, surveys and other interruptions. They want to solve their problem easily, so make it simple for them to buy your solution to their problem.

The "show me the money" features outlined above create a connection to your website. You also want to rank well for your keyword phrases so that you are found in the search engines. So how

---

[22] http://www.mmgyglobal.com as presented at SITE Florida Summit in Orlando, July 2012

do you keep your website clean, easy to navigate and full of relevant information? The answer is simple. You create a blog.

Blog

Your job as a guerrilla is to give website visitors an easy way to either buy what you are selling immediately or obtain the information they need to help them buy when they are ready. Your main website pages should give them the "stuff" they need to buy and your blog should give them the confidence that your business deserves to earn their hard-earned money.

If someone is not aware of your business website, then you need to "convince" the search engines to show your content when people search for what you offer and this is where the beauty happens. When you create great content, using your keyword phrases, you can attract people that are looking for what you offer while you give the search engines the fresh content that they look for. When you also provide ways to share your great content and comment about it - and you respond promptly and consistently – this is when the magic happens. Website visitors engage which provides social proof and search engines "see" fresh content and engagement, thus deeming the content to be valuable to their customers.

For example, if you operate a tour company, write about what your guests are doing, what you saw that day, history about the destination or interesting facts. Your blog content should be easy to read or watch and understand and it should be about one specific topic. You can choose to do video blogs, podcasts or written blogs. You will know which are preferred when you look at the engagement that occurs with the posts, so operate within the format that your audience prefers.

You should have a regular blog schedule, so that your audience knows when to look for new content. (In Part Four of this book there are exercises to help you define your blog topics and blog schedule.) Some blogs post multiple times a day, others post daily. I prefer to post once a week, although I have struggled to keep up this schedule while writing this book. One of the benefits of blogging is that it gives you a platform to brand yourself as an expert in your field. You can answer questions and provide valuable information about your industry, destination, business, products and services. It is important to use the keywords that relate to your business in your posts for optimal results. Treat each post as if it were original web content and be sure to include a CTA at the end.

If you are not able to add a blog to your current corporate website then create a stand-alone blog, with a keyword-rich domain name and link it to your corporate website including a link from your corporate website back to your blog. It is not as effective as having the blog attached to your website but you can still connect with your customers and potential customers. I recommend WordPress, http://wordpress.org, to our clients as it is a robust, easy-to-use platform that is well supported by developers throughout the world.

How to Use Your Blog as a Hub for Multi-Channel Marketing

Your blog is where you will share your expertise, thought leadership and where you will either subtly or not-so-subtly sell your products and services (subtly is better.). Your blog will be part of your main website or it will be a standalone blog, depending on the way your website was created. A Wordpress website includes a blog component whereas custom-built websites may not. Either way, ensure that you link your blog to your main website and include a CTA such as "book now" or "sign-up now". You will use your keyword phrases in your blog posts and I recommend that you include at least two images meant for sharing on social sites like Pinterest and Facebook.

Your Blog as a Hub

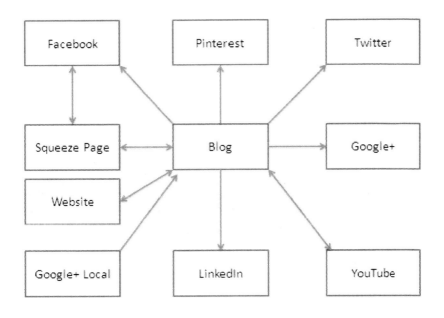

http://CarolWain.com

1. Create blog posts using your keyword phrases, images intended for sharing and content that is appreciated by your audience;

2. Take one of your most valuable insights from within your blog post (for example, a sentence or phrase that would be considered to be a "sound bite" on radio or TV) set-up a link to "Tweet this" using a service like ClickToTweet;

3. Share your blog post on your Facebook Page and pick your most interesting image to feature in the post (do not use 3rd party applications as they are not being "treated" as well in Facebook as a manual post);

4. On your Facebook page, give people a reason to opt-in to your mobile and/or email list via a squeeze page;

5. Tweet your Facebook Page post;

6. Pin your Facebook image to Pinterest;

7. Take your next most compelling image and pin it directly to Pinterest (linking back to your blog post);

8. Take a video posted to YouTube and embed it in your blog; then post on Facebook by linking to the video (otherwise the video may not play);
9. Post your video to Pinterest;
10. Take your entire Blog post and publish it to Google+, formatting the headline with Bold and adding an image;
11. If your blog post is particularly valuable, add the link to your Google+ Local page; and
12. Rinse and repeat.

Note: the day before I wrote this, I took an image from one of our directories (Cancunresorts.tv) and pinned it to Pinterest. Within twelve hours the image was repinned 24 times, with each of those images linking back to the directory. I will continue to use this technique, with our clients, for as long as it works. After all, pinning other people's stuff is much more "socially acceptable" than pinning your own stuff.

Images and Graphics

Remember that approximately half the population is right-brained and love pictures. Those beautiful images of sandy beaches, white duvets and fluffy pillows, spas and delicious looking dishes evoke our emotions and help us to long for that experience. Having images and graphics on your website is crucial because they help convey your message to your ideal customers as well as improve search engine rankings.

When you add an image to your website, Google will index the image in Google Images with the keywords that you have used to describe it. Use your keywords when naming your images (for example seattleveganrestaurant.jpg); creating your image description (Signature vegan dish at XYZ Restaurant in Seattle); deciding your alt tag (the words that someone will see if their device does not load images, for example, "Vegan Spaghetti Extraordinaire at XYZ Restaurant Seattle'; and even the image name. Be sure to watermark your images so they remain connected to your business even after they are shared on social media sites.

Many people "borrow" images from Google for presentations, websites, homework and other commercial and non-commercial purposes. Years ago, I thought that Google Images was a goldmine that I could use as I saw fit. It has taken me years to go through all of my "stock photos" to try to determine which ones I "borrowed" and which ones I have a license to use. Do not be tempted to borrow photos from the internet. It is not worth it and it is usually copyright infringement. Instead buy photos with a license to use them for what you intend to use them for; take your own photos; hire someone to create original works for you (and be sure they assign the copyright/watermark); or use creative-common-license photos that permit you to use the image as you intend. Always be sure to give the appropriate credit when using images that you have not created yourself and check that the license you have purchased covers your intended use.

Email Marketing

Email marketing has been a favorite tool for marketers and spammers alike for years because it is as close to "free" as it can get. The challenges are building your email marketing list, getting your emails opened and having people follow through with your CTA.

In addition to having an opt-in page on your website, you can also build your list by using contests, sweepstakes, Facebook promotions, in-store promotions and entering into fusion marketing arrangements (which I discuss in a later chapter). You can have an email list or a mobile list but it is preferable to have a list that includes both the email and the mobile contact information. List building and maintaining a healthy relationship with your list is important because:

- You absolutely want to build a community of raving supporters. To do that you need to communicate with them. To communicate you need to have an email and/or a mobile phone number;
- If you need to make some money today, the best way to do that is by sending a promotion to your list (mobile, email and social media community). Traditional advertising just cannot cut it when it comes to direct response marketing that converts to sales today;
- In the social media chapter I explain the value of social media. Social media is a great tool for growing communities, engaging customers and increasing profits. However, you do not exercise any control over those sites. You are at the mercy of Facebook, Twitter, LinkedIn, Foursquare, Yelp etc. but you do have control over your own list. Even if the social media

website shuts down your page because you breached one of their Terms of Service, you still have your list; and

- If you sell through meeting planners, travel agents, tour operators or other channel partners, create multiple lists and let them opt-in to the lists that appeal to their interests. The tourism industry is notorious for adding people to their lists and then spamming them with emails that are neither timely nor relevant. Spamming will get you in serious trouble with the authorities while you annoy those that you email; and

- Your list could potentially be more valuable than your business when the time comes to sell your business. A prospective buyer will look at your physical and virtual business, your financial statements and your customer list. A smart prospective buyer will also want to see how engaged your community is and your prospect list. You can "wow" them when you say that you have a list of 10,000 people and when you email or text message them it results in a spike of sales.

Your list's value is in the relationships you build, so create your list and provide so much education and entertainment that your customers and prospects look forward to reading what you send out.

How to get Your Emails Opened

The average open rates are all over the board, which is to be expected since there are so many variables.

To maximize your email marketing, you should always test two or more variations (called a "split-test").

Test:

- Subject lines;
- Offers;
- CTAs (note that if you are asking the reader to click on a link in the email, use three links – one near the top; one in the middle and one in the P.S.);
- Your message length;
- Your tone;
- Your words; and
- The timing when you send the message.

Keep testing one email against the other.

- Segment your lists;
- Segment between personality types, as outlined in Guerrilla Selling Chapter;
- Segment between those who have purchased and those who have not; and
- Segment between old list and new list (new list generally responds better).

Treat your list as the valuable commodity that it is.

I have listed some resources to help you manage your mailing lists and your campaigns on the Resources section of my website at http://carolwain.com

Search Engines Compared to Yellow Pages

Search engines are better than the old-fashioned Yellow Pages for a number of reasons:

- You have much more flexibility in how you present your business message and information through the search engines;
- Your costs will be much less than what you would pay for an ad in the print version of the Yellow Pages, particularly when you place larger ads;
- With local search marketing, you can update or make changes to your ads as often as you want. Compare that to a print ad that can only be changed annually;
- The internet also gives you a much larger reach than the traditional Yellow Pages directories, which are generally distributed once a year, and only to households that have landline phones. According to a study conducted by the Department of Health and Human Services at the National Center for Health Statistics[23] from July to December, 2010, approximately 29.7 percent of all adults live in households with only wireless phones (up 3.1 percent from the first 6 months of 2010). They have given up landlines completely. That means nearly one third of your target market may not

---

[23] http://www.cdc.gov/nchs/data/nhis/earlyrelease/wireless201106.htm

even receive a Yellow Pages directory. They rely on the internet for virtually 100 percent of their searches.

- According to Harris Interactive[24], sixty percent of those surveyed use the internet to find contact information, which will to continue to rise in correlation with the adoption of smart phones and location based services (LBS). In the same Harris Interactive survey, approximately seventy percent of adults in the U.S. "rarely or never" use the phone book.

Search Engine Marketing

Search Engine Marketing (SEM) means using the search engines to help you to market your business. It includes on-page SEO, where the text, videos, keywords and images on the website are manipulated to produce better results in the Search Engines Results Page (SERP). Off-page SEO is a little like popularity contests because the focus is on getting as many high-quality links back to your website as possible. The more back-links you have, the more popular your content or so the theory goes. The issue with off-page SEO is people who manipulate the search engines with questionable tactics to get those back-links. If you are paying someone to increase your off-page SEO be sure that they only use "white hat" SEO techniques, otherwise one day you could find your top ranked page somewhere in the online equivalent of Siberia.

One great way to get back links to your website is to include a social media bar that lets people Tweet, Pin, Like, Comment, Share, and otherwise connect what they read on your website to another website for the purposes of sharing your content.

The other component of SEM is paid advertising. I spoke with Rob Warner of http://ppcprofits.co.uk about the work that he is doing with his clients as it relates to paid search engine marketing. The interview can be found at http://carolwain.com.

> *"We work with a number of hotels. Regardless of the hotel, they have the same problem: the online booking agents or online travel agencies (OTAs). Those OTAs dominate the market in terms of market share; in terms of TV advertising; media advertising; and online advertising and they have the*

[24]http://readwrite.com/2011/01/20/study-confirms-death-of-phone-books

big budgets. The problem the hotels have is these sites take huge commissions. They are very, very expensive for the hotels and restaurants. One of my clients is a restaurant as well. Even they find that the online service is taking commissions from them.

They cost them a lot of money. They have a love-hate relationship with them I think. I think they like the bookings. They like the fact that they can put people in the hotel, but they know there are cheaper ways of getting those same people into the hotel.

We are able to reach the people that they would not otherwise reach, using AdWords. That Is a nIce way to put the control back in the hands of the hotels.

Every hotel is different but it is about looking at the specific things that a hotel is really good at. It might be location that is their main differentiator. One of my clients is a hotel near Heathrow Airport, UK's largest airport. It is quite a nice hotel. You can imagine how competitive that marketplace is. Every spare space and piece of land has got a hotel on it, trying to cash in on the biggest airport in the country.

We advertise on the fact that it is close to Heathrow. We are advertising on the fact that it is a four-star hotel. Most of the Heathrow Airport hotels tend to be lower market and essentially cheaper. We quite specifically focus on those kind of people that are looking for a four-star hotel at Heathrow. We know for example that if it is a UK person searching for it, they will typically be searching for Heathrow parking. If it is an American person searching for it, they will typically be searching for LHR hotels, being the airline code for London Heathrow. We know that if we run an ad for in the US using LHR language rather than Heathrow it has a better appeal. We have to know where their customers typically would come from. If you are flying to Tokyo or San Francisco, when you have got a 12 or 13 hour flight or further, you may well stay down the night before, either end of your travel, so we are advertising that way. If you have an hour's flight to Paris, you will not likely stay the night.

I always say a good AdWords campaign is like a vending machine that you continually get a consistent rate of money coming out either end of it, but if you are not testing, it is like a gamble. You do not know what is going to happen. On the ad level we test two things at a time. We will work on a grid where we will have two headlines and two body copies. Each headline will have each variation of the body copy and vice versa. We have room for four ads at any time and then pick the winner, or you can pick the two winners. There is usually a winning headline, but there is less clarity between the body copy. Then when we have got that one and we do the test, and another test. The difference between a good ad and a bad ad will be huge. We have got ads that converts one percent for a keyword, and an ad for the same keyword that will converts at ten percent. It is a difference between a good campaign and a bad campaign is your targeting and the quality of ad copy.

The first piece of advice that I would give is, if you are thinking of doing it, and you have a Google representative and they offer to do it for you, do not let them. Google reps are very nice people but they set up campaigns in ways that suit Google primarily. That is not the way we would ever set a campaign up. I think one crazy thing to think about is a starting point, which most people do not think about is, start with your own brand name.

People who are vaguely aware of you will still type the name of your hotel in the search bar even if they know the name of your website. If you do not come up on that search an OTA will be bidding on your brand name. Make sure you bid on your own brand name. It is usually really, really cheap, and it is the single biggest source of conversions you will get.

Once you have done that, look at location related things and think about it from the point of view of what are you nearby? If you are near a tourist attraction, you might want to advertise on that, for example, "Houses of Parliament Hotel" or "Palace Hotel".

You are picking out the things that are nearby. If you are a tourist coming into the area, you know you want something near, for example, Buckingham Palace. Look for local landmarks that you can signpost a reference uses of. That same applies to restaurants and other tourist attractions as well. You can quite easily leverage off these things. Obviously we can narrow it down to focus on your star rating.

In Google AdWords you can have something called ad extensions; which are basically extra links under the main body of your text, which you can choose whatever you want to put on them, and they just make your Google AdWords larger.

If you are advertising a hotel or a restaurant you do not know why people are looking for you. If someone is searching for a London restaurant, they could be a businessman wanting to take a client out for a meal; a couple wanting a weekend away; or a family doing a trip to the theater. You do not know. You can use those ad extensions to put different calls to action, or message out there to see what people are coming for. If someone is looking for a London hotel, all you know is they are after a hotel but if you put something in there to say specifically, 'romantic weekend', 'corporate discounts', or whatever else, they will resonate with that, apart from the fact that they want a hotel in London. If they want a hotel in London for their business trip, it will relate to the person looking for it specifically. Google normally shows between four and six extensions but sometimes if your ad is really good and gets good click-through-rate (CTR), you can get eight extensions shown at once. Fundamentally Google wants to show ads that gets clicks. If your ad gets a CTR better than anybody else and your bid price is right, you will get the click.

The two most common mistakes by far are:

- Making extensive use of broad match keywords. There are different types of matching that you can use when people type words into the search engine. Broad match is exactly what it says. It is very, very broad. You come up with the widest possible number of searches. The downside is a huge proportion of the traffic you get will be utter rubbish, and of no interest to you whatsoever, but you will still get charged if it gets clicked. You have to make sure wherever *possible to use exact match and phrase match, and sometimes what we call modified broad match. If you use modified broad match and phrase, use negative keywords as well. We do that once a day to add negative keywords like jobs, careers, vacancies, recruitment, salary, all those kinds of things that you do not want your hotel or restaurant ad to show up for.*

- *The second biggest mistake is people have huge campaigns that are not broken down at all. You need to make your campaigns as micro-focused as you possibly can. If you do not do that again you will struggle. You will spend a lot of money that you do not need to. To continue with the London hotel example, you could, I would say put in bids for the keyword "hotel London". That is a hugely generic expression that covers everything from a one-star bed and breakfast on the outskirts of London, through to a five-star hotel in Sensory. It could be anything. The chances of your hotel being absolutely right for that search and then likely to spend money with you are pretty remote. If you are bidding on that kind of keyword, expect to lose a lot of money with it, be prepared to.*

If on the other hand you are saying, you run a campaign for five-star hotels in the west end. That is very specific. If someone is searching for that, if you are a five-star hotel and you are in the west end, you have got a pretty good chance. I would encourage everybody to break their offer into as many small chunks as they possibly can, and think why is that person searching, and create a little campaign for each of those individual searches.

If someone is looking for a hotel close to a theater, for example, and you have a hotel close to a theater, create a theater based campaign and use theater language in your ads. If you are also a five-star, do a five-star campaign focusing on those kinds of keywords. The person looking for the five-star hotel and the person looking for the theater hotel want different things. They may both be your hotel. You have to use the language they are using to provide the ads for them.

Our hotel clients, we typically see 10 - 15 and as high as 20 times return on our spending in terms of bookings. That is a number not to be sniffed at. I think most hotels would be thrilled with that compared to the commissions they pay. It is possible. That is not because we are particularly brilliant. I think we are quite good. I am sure other people could go out and with the right kind of application get that result for themselves.

One final tip, which people should be aware of, well two really, test everything all the time and keep going. The second is to bear in mind if you are trying to attract out of area visitors, back to the comments made earlier, make sure you understand the language they are searching in. It may even not be your spoken language. You may have to have translations done."

Internet Marketing Challenges

The internet is a double-edged sword for tourism. On the one hand it makes reaching potential customers a lot easier and faster. It also enables you to track campaigns and CTRs, and you can communicate with your customers and prospects a lot easier. The other side is that the internet has forever changed the way consumers book travel. I was a travel agent as the industry was changing, first to zero or reduced commissions, then to direct sales. Today tourism businesses are finding that technology has evolved so that the consumer does not even need to shop directly from the supplier's website.

The metasearch engine, (an aggregator of databases that presents all results from various search engines and databases together), is a tool that travelers use to research for the best pricing. According to Peter Yesawich, Vice Chairman of MMGY Global, during a presentation at the SITE Florida Summit in Orlando July 2012, 27 percent of travelers have used a metasearch engine. While this number is still a minority of travelers, hoteliers and airlines need to understand that price shopping is much easier than it used to be.

Other game-changing websites enable travelers to:

Buy through private sale and collective buying websites

- http://www.sniqueaway.com is a TripAdvisor company. *"For the first time private sale meets crowd-sourcing approval on a brand new members-only website where each offer is endorsed by the people. All hotels featured on SniqueAway have earned a minimum four-star rating and a four or five out of five review rating on TripAdvisor."*
- http://www.tripalertz.com – *"Have your product spread throughout the virtual universe. Because the price decreases as more travelers sign up, buyers have an incentive to do the marketing for you."*

Buy using a competitive bidding website

- http://www.biddingtraveler.com/ *"Priceline bidding help and tools. If you are bidding for travel, we will tell you what to bid for hotels, winning bids, hotel lists, even rejected bids. Just search and see."*
- http://betterbidding.com *"Priceline and Hotwire Hotel Bidding, Help and Advice"*
- http://backbid.com/ *"BackBid is a hotel booking website that revolutionizes how travelers book hotel rooms. BackBid empowers you, the traveler, to find the best possible hotel room, for the best price, with no elaborate or time-consuming searches necessary. By posting your existing hotel reservation to BackBid, hotels are able to see your travel plans and offer bids for your business, offering either discounts or value-added services, like upgraded rooms, free parking or breakfast"*.

See pricing transparency

- http://tingo.com is a TripAdvisor company *"that automatically rebooks travelers at the lower rate if their hotel drops its price – and then automatically refunds the difference to their credit card."*

Comparison shop

- http://www.kayak.com/ -- is a metasearch engine *"...easily compare hundreds of travel sites at once...we give you choices where to book... We also offer travel management tools including an itinerary management tool, flight status updates and price alerts"*
- http://www.dealbase.com/ -- metasearch engine *"the largest collection of flight and hotel deals and discount offers on the planet."*
- http://fly.com *"Fly.com is an airfare search engine that makes looking for airfares both quick and easy. When you use Fly.com, the website searches hundreds of airline and major travel sites for real-time fares, and then presents the results in a simple, clean and easy-to-understand format. We even include taxes in the fare prices so you can quickly see the total cost."*
- http://www.yapta.com/ *"Yapta aims to help travelers get a better handle on pricing by providing easy-to-use tools and information that assures they get the best value from their travel spending."*

Google is also making a play into travel planning. It already has a hotel booking and flight booking engine in some markets and they are exploring a complete travel booking engine that can create complex itineraries using sources that the current websites cannot or do not offer (for example, combining discount carriers, legacy carriers, buses and trains).

One of the biggest challenges to hoteliers is not actually the independent (FIT) traveler that uses these new websites to lower vacation expenses. Instead, if corporate travel departments start to use these sites, the lucrative business travel market will be under attack. If savvy meeting planners and travel managers band together and start to negotiate group rates and corporate rates based on pricing that is offered through a group social buy or deal website, or if a service like BackBid.com or Tingo.com starts catering to the corporate market, profits will evaporate for travel suppliers.

Since prices are more transparent, your brand clarity becomes more urgent. You need to ensure that you have a truly unique selling proposition (USP) . You also need to pay attention to how you can increase your core value and you need to ensure that you carve out your own "Blue Ocean" strategy. (See "Defining Your Value Story" chapter).

Groupon

At first I was completely opposed to Groupon... after all the economics do not make sense for the merchant and, if done wrong, the impact on cash flow can be devastating.

I have heard two stories (interestingly both were related to dental care) that used Groupon successfully. One dentist created an "at-home" whitening kit which he sold via Groupon. If people wanted extra kits they were at regular prices. He could also sell this product nationally, yet if the buyer was local, she could also come into the office for professional treatment. I like this example because the main cost was in creating and distributing the kits, so it was highly scalable.

The other was for a dentist that also offered teeth whitening in the office and then upsold another appointment or a product during the initial visit. This dentist knew that a small percentage would repeat but it made sense to her to use Groupon to increase her patient count. Teeth whitening is, apparently, a high margin product, so I can see how this would work.

I am still not a huge fan of these types of sites but I can see how it could work for many business types if – and only if – the plan is well thought out. Understand that some regular customers will buy the Groupon and many Groupon customers have no intention of returning when they buy. In this instance, using Groupon can be a very expensive branding exercise, particularly if there is not a plan in place to give customers an offer to return.

If I were running a Groupon campaign, I would want to know which customers are coming to my business with a Groupon in hand as they entered my business. I would track how many people are new customers versus existing customers. I would train my staff to explain the competitive advantages of shopping with us (how many businesses ever do that?) and to explain our business and what we offer.

At the point of sale, I would have an offer for them to join our "Club" by giving us their email or a mobile phone number in exchange for specials and exclusive invites or deals. Personalized service will blow the bargain shopper away because they are used to being treated as bargain hunters. Furthermore, those that liked the experience enough to consider returning will be more likely to give their email / mobile phone number for more value-added services, special promotions etc. The value is always in the relationship with your list and as long as you are building a list and impressing the customer, Groupon may work for you.

For the customers who shop without a Groupon, make them an offer too. Hand-out a scratch and win card, a free appetizer card or a loyalty punch card with extra credits for purchase. At the point of sale, extend an invitation to join your "Club".

I created a daily deal calculator, which was intended for personal use. However, if you would like a copy of it, please go to http://carolwain.com/is-groupon-good-for-your-business/ and subscribe by providing your name and email address. Once you have done that, and you confirm your subscription, you will get the calculator and an explanation of how it works.

The two biggest factors when contemplating the use of a daily deal service are your initial offer and your follow-up plan to encourage repeat purchases.

I am not a fan of Groupon due to the financial implications but I am a fan of occasionally creating your own group deals or flash sales as long as they do not diminish your profit margins or train customers to only shop when the deal is on. When you create your own deal you save the thirty percent commission, control your discount and offer and you define the release date. Ensure the deal makes sense financially; the product or service is unique for the promotion and capture an email address or mobile number so that you can build your list to convince them to come back again without a deep discount.

Flash Sales

One way to offload rooms or seats (in planes, restaurants and tours) is to hold a flash sale. A flash sale is a time-limited offer, available online, that includes steep discounts to move inventory quickly. A flash sale is perceived by the customer to be a great value, while the business owner can sell inventory that may have gone unsold.

There is a culture of impatience in our society and one of the ways that you can use it to your advantage is by giving your customers a highly-valuable reason to opt-in to your email list and your mobile list, namely they will be the first to hear about a flash sale.

JetBlue Airways uses flash sales to fill seats and encourage customers to make a decision about a travel purchase within a very short time frame. The beauty of the flash sale is that customers do not expect to receive an email with a flash sale at any given time, yet many buy when they receive it. What a great way to use psychology to move excess inventory and to fill seats or beds.

Imagine if you received an email with a fantastic offer for a trip that you had not even thought about during a time that you had not considered taking a vacation. If the deal looks appealing and you have flexibility in your schedule, you would immediately contact your potential travel partner, share the deal and start talking about whether you could get away during this time. Within hours you could be booked to go on a trip that you had no intention of going on when you woke up. According to MMGY Global[25] 28 percent of travelers have booked a trip with less than six days until departure and 14 percent of travelers have purchased a travel service as a result of an unexpected email. If it makes sense for your business, test the effectiveness of your own flash sale.

Social media also plays a huge part in sharing flash sales. As I was searching for flash sale examples, I came across websites where people were sharing a deal from JetBlue that was announced on March 31, 2012.

On one website[26] there were 60 interactions between 9:41 A.M. and 1:21 P.M. about this particular flash sale and how to make the most of it.

> *"Promo code SAVE200 is good today only for 3 hours from 12 P.M. – 3 P.M. ET.*
>
> *Get $200 off the new purchase of a JetBlue Getaways vacation package of 3+ nights originating from the continental U.S. to*

[25] http://mmgyglobal.com
[26] http://slickdeals.net/f/4674886-JetBlue-Three-Hour-Flash-Sale-with-200-OFF-a-3-Night-Vacation-Package-Travel-to-Caribbean-Mexico-or-Florida

the Caribbean, Mexico or Florida for travel June 1, 2012 through December 31, 2012.[27]"

Flash sales, whether for trips or for meals, will continue to be a win-win way to offload inventory, while ensuring that your emails are opened and your customers and prospects engage with your brand. Used infrequently, to avoid expectations for discounts, and in conjunction with a strong brand message and core values, you can avoid devaluing your brand while impressing your customers.

Conclusion

The internet has changed the way people research and shop for many products and services and tourism is perhaps the largest industry to be both positively and negatively impacted. The OTAs are a double-edged sword as they bring business that you may not have otherwise earned but the commissions are high; the metasearch engines make comparison shopping easy for the consumer while it puts pressure on pricing; and the group deal sites are great for exposure but they could be very expensive If you do not have a follow-up plan.

To counteract this, you need to have a well designed, easy-to-navigate website which gives visitors the information they are looking for. You need great content – using your keyword phrases – that is updated frequently to attract search engines, prospects and customers. If you invest in search engine marketing it is possible to attract customers that may otherwise buy from an OTA. Capturing contact information is essential so that you can follow up by phone, text messaging, direct mail and email. Most importantly, remember that although internet marketing may become a large part of your marketing plan it should not be your sole marketing weapon as a variety of weapons works best.

---

[27] http://dealspl.us/Travel-and-Tickets_deals/p_jetblue-three-hour-flash-sale-with-off-3-night

Chapter 9 – Local Marketing

"One way to sell a consumer something in the future is simply to get his or her permission in advance."

Seth Godin

The term "Local Marketing" has many definitions, depending on who you ask including the following:

- Store-specific promotions;
- Local-area merchandising;
- Local media advertising;
- Direct marketing to specific neighborhoods;
- Marketing to your local community;
- Marketing your community to non-residents; and
- Using Google Maps and Google+ Local to market your business.

Since the tourism industry comprises sectors that include restaurants, travel agents, golf courses and recreational activities that cater to local area customers together with meeting planners, cruise lines, tour operators, car rental companies and transportation companies that move people; as well as DMCs, DMOs and accommodations businesses that market to in the in-bound traveler. I will explore them all.

Local Area Marketing

According to Google, 20 percent of all searches are related to location[28] and 40 percent of browser-based mobile search[29] has a local or offline intent. More than 18.2 billion searches[30] were conducted in December 2011 up 2 percent) with Google Sites ranking first with 12 billion searches (up 3 percent). This means approximately 2.4 billion searches were related to location - in other words, local search. The bottom line is that more and more people are using the internet to search for local information.

---

[28] http://www.huffingtonpost.com/andy-plesser/googles-marissa-mayer-loc_b_867664.html
[29] http://searchengineland.com/study-suggests-50-percent-local-search-happening-in-apps-113283
[30] http://www.comscore.com/Insights/Press_Releases/2012/1/comScore_Releases_December_2011_U.S._Search_Engine_Rankings

If your business has ideal customers that work, play or live within a certain radius from your business, your marketing needs to be highly targeted towards your local community. Your approach to marketing could include email marketing, mobile marketing, social media marketing, referrals, reputation and review management, special events, community building activities, creative direct response mail, surveying your customers, sending thank you cards and holiday cards, personalized service and depending on your audience, radio and newspaper ads but only if they have an irresistible offer with a CTA that captures names, emails or mobile phone numbers. Your job is to get into the minds of your customers and prospects so that you are considered each time someone in your local area intends to buy what you sell.

You need to regularly read and respond to reviews on websites such as Foursquare, TripAdvisor, Yelp, Urban Spoon and other check-in and review sites. You should be looking at the check-ins on Facebook and the reviews there and you should be watching out for mentions on Twitter.

Guerrillas know that creativity and multiple-channels of marketing are keys to enticing local customers to come to your business repeatedly, so put on your thinking cap and look at unique and profitable ways to fill your cash register.

Google+ Local

Google+ Local replaced Google Places in May 2012. The premise behind Google+ Local is that people will recommend businesses to others in their circles by writing reviews and uploading photos. When this is combined with reviews from other sources, videos, photos, a strong keyword-rich description, business address, phone number and location on Google Maps, it is a powerful and free marketing tool.

Businesses that have good reviews and complete information will have a far greater likelihood of being chosen when someone searches for that type of business and I encourage you to claim or create then optimize your page. If you have not yet created a Google+ personal profile and a Google+ Business Page create them at the same time because the more places that Google can find you and your business, the better.

Attracting Visitors to Your Business

When you rely on visitors for your sales, your marketing approach is different because the visitor needs to be aware of the destination first and that responsibility typically lies with a governmental division or department. While I have seen many fantastic marketing strategies and campaigns created by DMOs, there are DMOs that simply should not be in charge of marketing a destination because they are not producing the results that the tourism businesses need. These DMOs need to read this book so that they learn how to define their ideal customers and create value differentiators. They can go about building communities and using fusion marketing and use multi-channel marketing to increase the number of visitors for their tourism related businesses.

If your business is fortunate to be represented by a great DMO, the next step is to establish yourself as the best local business for the ideal customers you have identified. The most common ways are through outbound marketing such as trade shows, memberships, networking events, conferences, direct mail, emails, fam trips, sales rep phone calls, magazine and newspaper ads and TV and radio spots and inbound marketing where people find you through your website, social media accounts, Google+ Local and Google maps. As someone on the receiving side of this marketing, I see a tremendous loss of opportunity and wasted money because the messages are not written for "me", they don't have a compelling offer, a sense of urgency and a CTA that makes me want to act. Be sure to write to your ideal customer in a way that resonates and encourages them to act as you wish.

Other Marketing Weapons

In other chapters within this book you will find advice for using email, mobile marketing, social media marketing, fusion marketing, community building and traditional media. You will find the mix that works best for you by testing different guerrilla marketing weapons and different promotions. Whatever you do, think about what the customer wants before you think about what you want and you will have a lot more success driving locals and visitors to your business.

Get Creative

The City of Richmond, BC is running an awareness campaign where a blogger (who receives a salary of $50,000, a gym membership and a $30 per day dining stipend) dines out at restaurants in the city every day for 365 days. The blog, which can be found at http://www.365daysofdining.com/, is meant to draw attention to the many dining choices available within the city. While the blog is intended to be valuable to tourists, it is also of value to people who live in the city.

1n 2009, Tourism Queensland launched a "Best Job in the World" campaign that drew international media attention and 200,000 unique visitors to their website in the first 24 hours which crashed its server. Eventually a man from the UK was chosen as the winner for the glamorous 6-month "Island Caretaker" position which required him to explore the Great Barrier Reef Islands and report his experience via weekly blogs, video updates and photo diaries.

What could you do to draw attention to your community and the tourism businesses within it?

Chapter 10 – Social Media Marketing

"In a way, the Web is like your Hollywood agent: it speaks for you whenever you are not around to comment."

Chris Brogan

Guerrillas know that engagement and relationship building are critical to success. They also look for ways to increase their profits with low-cost and innovative methods. Social media marketing fits all these criteria and it is particularly useful with businesses in the tourism industry. Social media marketing also provides social proof, which is extremely important for converting prospects to customers.

Let us start by defining social media versus social networking: social media is the communication channel to share information, in the same way that TV is media. Social networking is the process of two-way communication and relationship building that happens on social networking sites. It is like networking in person except it happens online.

Your social media presence is also used by Google for the search engine results page.

The top 10 social networking sites[31] for October 2012 are

1. Facebook
2. Twitter
3. LinkedIn
4. MySpace
5. Google+
6. Deviant Art
7. Live Journal
8. Tagged
9. Orkut
10. Pinterest

---

[31] http://www.ebizmba.com/articles/social-networking-websites

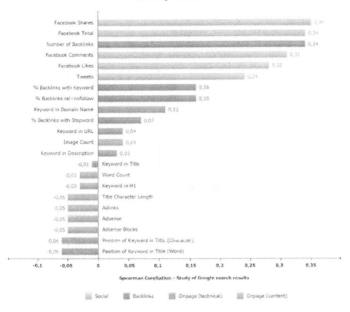

Ranking Factors UK

Spearman Correlation - Study of Google search results

Social · Backlinks · Onpage (technical) · Onpage (content)

A study by SearchMetrics[32] shows that social signals from Facebook, Twitter and Google+ now correlate with good rankings in Google's index.

Social media marketing is still in its infancy, with some marketers reluctant to take the leap, some early adopters pulling back and many marketers not quite sure why or even how best to use social networking sites.

Because social media marketing is still fairly new there is not one set of metrics to determine ROI. However, you can measure results if you have specific objectives defined before you start. Are you looking to increase your profits, exposure or traffic or engagement? If you are looking to increase your profits, then your campaign will be created using a CTA that is all about buying what you sell. (Try to keep promotional posts to approximately 20 percent of all posts you make.) You can track how many clicks and how many sales you realized based on that campaign.

---

[32] http://www.searchmetrics.com/en/white-paper/google-ranking-factors-uk-2012/

If you want to increase exposure, you can create images intended for sharing on Pinterest and Facebook. You can create a contest or sweepstakes and use Facebook to market it. You may decide that Groupon is a good way to gain massive amounts of exposure, (its best benefit) although the price may be too steep if you do not have a solid plan to get people to return.

If your objective is to increase traffic, what type of traffic? Traffic to your physical business? Your event? Your website etc.? If it is traffic to your website you can check your analytics to measure the effect. If it is traffic to your Facebook page, then you can check the Facebook Insights (http://facebook.com/insights). If it is traffic to your business, you can track the number of people that come in because of the campaign.

Traffic, for the sake of traffic, means very little. You want targeted traffic, especially your ideal customer type of traffic because ultimately you want profitable sales. Choose your promotions wisely so you only attract the type of traffic you want. For example, there is very little point of giving away the latest phone or tablet in a consumer promotion because you will attract people who simply want to win that prize rather than those who could be a potential customer. However, if you have a promotion intended to drive meeting planner-only traffic, that prize would make sense as planners use both daily.

Engage With Your Customers

Social networking is the process of two-way communications and relationship building that takes place on social networking sites. It is like networking in person except it happens online. You can engage with your customers by responding promptly to their queries via Facebook and Twitter. You can resolve issues before they start to fester and make their way onto a permanent review website. You can surprise your customers with a gift, as you will see in the KLM example a little later in this chapter. You can interact with them on your Facebook page and let them be "heard". You can crowd-source and ask for suggestions for an upcoming product or promotion. You can give your followers and fans the inside scoop on any announcements. You can make them part of a VIP club. The potential is limitless. Again, social media is a guerrilla marketer's dream tool... or it could be a nightmare.

As I mentioned in an earlier chapter, each and every person associated with your business is in marketing. When that person takes their interactions online to social networking and review sites the impact is far greater than one-on-one interactions offline. The people that formally represent you online need to be thoroughly trained with guidelines about what they can and cannot do and say. They need to be given scenarios that could occur and how they should respond. They need to be trained in the proper way to interact and the tone that they should take. They need to know what, why and how to take conversations offline and they need to be thoroughly trained in dealing with trolls (people that thrive on creating chaos in online communities) and situations that suddenly explode. As you saw with the Thomas Cook example, there is potential for disaster or a great publicity opportunity, so training and monitoring is key.

Here are some of the highlights from a few of the more popular social networking sites.

Google+

Google+ is a relatively new social network that permits people and businesses to create pages, add people to their "circles", follow people and pages, post news and images and create "hangouts". The jury is still out on whether this is a useful social network and whether it will give Facebook a run for its money. However, it is a Google product and if you want "Google Love", I encourage you to embrace it. In 2011, I created a post about Google+ that I included on our blog and announced on Google+. That post was indexed and appeared in the search engines within an hour.

I recommend that after you create a blog post on your website, copy your entire blog post into Google+ (up to 100,000 characters) as this gives Google more content to index while ultimately sending people back to your website through your CTAs and the links in your blog post.

Another way to use Google+ is to "+1" something that you find. A "+1" is similar to a Facebook "like" or a Pinterest "pin". It is your way of saying that you like something, which Google will then use to send you similar content. Ask people to +1 your posts and +1 your own content too.

Pinterest

Pinterest is a social media website that people use to "pin" images and videos that they like to their "boards". Pinterest is a series of online scrapbooks which you create after you sign up for an account. Pinterest is a good news social media website because our tourism products are highly visual, shareable, and can tap emotions, such as desire. As I explained in the internet marketing chapter, I pinned a photo of a resort from our Cancun Resorts directory one evening as a test and it was re-pinned (by people I do not even know) 24 times over night. That image links back to our http://CancunResorts.tv website and it shows up as the source for the image.

Guerrilla marketers know that social media is about engaging in a two-way dialogue, so whatever you do, do not revert to sell, sell, sell. Be fun, be helpful and be inspirational with your images and they will be repinned. Also, ask your customers to pin images enjoying your spa, your meal, your golf course etc. and to include your business name.

Pinterest Contests and Sweepstakes

Some businesses choose to use Pinterest to offer a contest or a sweepstakes. FlyBMI created one of the first sweepstakes on Pinterest. The concept was not quite as simple as it could have been. FlyBMI uploaded 55 images to five boards for destinations that they fly to. They asked that people repin six images a week and they were going to draw six numbers, similar to a lottery. The problem is that choosing six numbers out of 55 is tough, as anyone who has played the lottery knows. So it appears that they changed the rules part way through and instead randomly drew one number for the image of the week. If you pinned the correct image you had a chance to win flights from the airline. Those odds were a lot better as a quick search of their boards shows that images have been repinned between 20 and 120 times. According to their website *"Over the past month and a half, we have received over 3,500 Repins, 650 followers across our 11 boards and a number of delighted winners of our free bmi flights."[33]*

As time goes on and people get used to using Pinterest, the engagement with Pinterest contests will increase, provided they are simple, fun and include decent odds of winning.

---

[33] http://bmisocialplanet.tumblr.com/post/18190160550/bmi-pinterest-lottery

Spa Week ran a contest that required pinners to:

> *"(1) Follow Spaweek on Pinterest;*
> *(2) Create a board and title it "My Dream Spa Retreat" then add a description answering the question "What does your dream spa retreat look like?";*
> *(3) Pin one of the ten spa images on Spa Week Daily's contest post as the foundation for your entry board (I am not sure what that means);*
> *(4) Include at least nine pins in your board;*
> *(5) Include #spaweek in the pin's description; and*
> *(6) Post the link to the board in the comments section of the original contest announcement pin, located in their "My Dream Spa Retreat Contest" board."*[34]

It appears that approximately 100 people participated "correctly" by creating the board with the correct name and the hashtag (#spaweek). A few others had the hashtag but not the correct board name and others had the correct board name but not the hashtag. However, only 21 people then put their pin on the original contest announcement pin[35].

As with every contest or sweepstakes, do not make it too difficult to engage participation. The more steps, the lower the engagement level. The simpler the conditions, the more exposure you can receive. After all, contests are typically used for increasing exposure and building your mailing lists.

Warning: You must be aware of "consideration" which cannot be part of any sweepstakes in the USA. Requiring people to have a computer and internet connection could be deemed to be "consideration". Requiring people to spend a lot of effort (for example time) could be deemed to be "consideration". Jay and I are not lawyers and we do not provide legal advice, so before you create a contest or sweepstakes check with your legal team for approval. There is a great post on Social Media Examiner[36] that is written by a lawyer, Sara

---

[34] http://www.spaweekblog.com/2012/03/14/pin-it-to-win-it-my-dream-spa-retreat-pinterest-contest/
[35] http://pinterest.com/pin/30117891228087570/
[36] http://www.socialmediaexaminer.com/social-media-promotions-and-the-law-what-you-need-to-know/

Hawkins, and she talks about contests, sweepstakes and lotteries as part of social media promotions.

Facebook

Facebook is a fantastic guerrilla marketing weapon because it can only cost you the time and energy that you put into creating and maintaining the page, which could be a few minutes a day up to many hours a day depending on your business. Optional add-ons include design work, ads or apps you may buy to enhance your Facebook presence and your engagement with your audience.

There are over one billion users on Facebook, and if you do not have a presence there you are missing out on potential business and engaging in a two-way dialogue with your customers and prospects. People expect that you have a Facebook Page, so much so, that if you have not created a Facebook Page where people can "check in" to your business, they can create one for you just by checking in at your location using their phone's GPS feature.

Before I provide an overview of Facebook, let us start with a few basic definitions as many people get tripped up with the terminology.

Profile: This is your personal account, for you as a person and not to be used for commercial purposes (according to Facebook's Terms of Service[37])

Page: This is the account for a local business or place; company, institution or organization; brand or product; artist, band or public figure; entertainment; and cause or community.

Newsfeed: This is what users see when they login to Facebook. It is their private feed containing updates from friends and pages that they engage with along with an increasing number of paid messages. Facebook users do not see all updates from friends, people they subscribed to or pages they like because Facebook filters the messages according to its algorithm called EdgeRank. If people share, comment and like a post EdgeRank "deems" it to be valuable and in turn more people see it. If engagement of a post is low, only a small percentage of users will see it in their newsfeed which is frustrating to both user and marketer.

---

[37] https://www.facebook.com/policies/

I didn't even know that there was a newsfeed for my various business pages until my friend, Joyce, told me. To see it you need to be logged into Facebook as your page and then you click on the word "Facebook" on the top left side or the home link on the right side of the page. In the Guerrilla Marketing Workbook, which you can find at http://carolwain.com, I take you step by step through how to do this and provide other tips for using Facebook.

Timeline: A timeline is a reverse chronological order history of posts shared by a specific person or organization. When you click on a friend's name or profile image you will be taken to their timeline. If you click on your own name (top right side of your profile page) you will be taken to your own timeline. You can control what appears on your timeline by tightening your privacy settings; deleting or hiding what you do not wish to show; and changing the settings for an individual post so that it is shown to whom you want it to be shown to. By default, you will see the timeline for your own page and the timeline for other pages when you visit them.

Your timeline is where you will post comments, images (lots of images) and videos to educate, entertain and enlighten your customers/prospects. You should remember that most people will see your posts in their newsfeed rather than by returning to your page after they like it, so always structure your posts so they look great in the newsfeed.

Only a small percentage of your posts will be shown to your followers as Facebook uses its EdgeRank algorithm to determine if it is "valuable". It is extremely important that you post high-value information that gets shared, commented on and liked. Less than 20 percent of all posts should be promotional in nature and you should ask questions and ask for feedback. Remember to ask/suggest to people what you would like them to do, for example "If you like this post, please share it".

Facebook Insights

You will want to keep an eye on your Facebook Insights, to see what types of posts people are engaging with and then you should create more posts like them. Facebook Insights gives you a lot of information about who has liked your page and the demographics. It also gives you data about where your new likes have come from, which is a very interesting statistic to me. As I write this section "People who liked your page from the Likes section of their own timeline or someone else's" has more than double the next highest source, which is, "People who liked the page on the page itself".

Facebook Messages

You can engage with your customers and prospects by permitting your community to send you messages (if you have enabled this option). I have seen fall-out with pages that have disabled the ability to message. People who are trying to reach a "real person" via your Facebook page and cannot connect with you may choose to post on your timeline instead.

Using Facebook for Push Marketing

Engagement has actually risen with many of the larger brands after the change to the new timeline, although I predict that it may decrease just as quickly if the platform turns into a great big marketing pitch. Facebook needs to increase its revenue (just like the rest of us) and it is doing so is by increasing the ways that marketers can pay to get their ads in front of people. There is a bit of a disconnect with the social aspect of Facebook, where the conversations are two-way and the discussions are about being helpful, entertaining and inquisitive versus the monetization of Facebook, which is about interruption marketing with Facebook ads and promoted posts, particularly when they appear in the newsfeed. If you have not yet found a genuine way to connect with your community put your time, energy and money into finding out how. Social networks come and go but the true value is in creating relationships with people that stick with you wherever that may be.

Facebook Contests and Sweepstakes

Facebook contests are a great way to increase engagement on your page and to grow your list. Unlike Pinterest, Facebook has many restrictions when it comes to running a contest, sweepstakes or competition. The terms related to running a contest or sweepstakes on Facebook are on the Facebook website, so I encourage you to read the latest version before creating a contest. Contests are great for list building so although Facebook's restrictions are extensive I recommend them. Be sure to offer a reward that appeals to your ideal customers without attracting the "I just want to win" people.

Overall, Facebook is a great place to engage your audience with very little expense, other than time and imagination. Regardless of the promotion you use, be sure to capture an email address and/or mobile phone number because the ultimate goal is to grow your list.

Facebook Groups

There are three types of Facebook Groups: open, closed and secret. Open groups can be found in a search for groups; they show the members of the group and what the members post. Closed groups can be found in a search for groups and they show the members but not the posts. Secret groups cannot be found in the search, nor can anyone except for members see who the other members are and what they post.

The exclusivity factor of a closed or secret group cannot be underestimated. I belong to secret groups and closed groups and they are tight communities who protect each other and openly share, knowing that what they say is for the benefit of the members. The psychological factor of being in a secret or closed group is huge so it is a great way to build relationships with your customers, your resellers/affiliates and your influencers.

Warning – if you create a closed or secret group be very careful about who you let in and promptly crack down on those who spam the newsfeed or members with self-serving promotions as the valuable members of the group will quickly lose interest and they will leave.

Twitter

Twitter is another social media website that you should consider. The point of Twitter is to post short updates (up to 140 characters at a time). It can be useful for sending out messages about special offers, announcing blog posts or promotions you are running but more importantly it is another way for your customers and potential customers to contact you.

Uses for Twitter

- Monitoring what is being said about your brand, your industry, your competitors;
- Customer service. (I noticed that BMI International is answering customer service requests on Twitter);
- Connecting with your potential clients;

- Showing thought leadership;
- A little bit of promotion (maximum of 20% of all tweets);
- Highlighting your blog posts;
- Attracting attendees to your event or tweet-up;
- And my absolute favorite…. What KLM did, which was to surprise passengers with gifts for passengers when they Tweeted about their KLM flight at Schipol Airport. It is a bit freaky to have someone approach you with a personal gift like muscle ointment when you are on your way to build homes for the disadvantaged in Mexico – as one passenger tweeted – but it is nice to be recognized as someone other than a name, passport and Passenger Name Record. To see the smiles on the passengers' faces when they realized that they received special attention (and more legroom, in the case of one passenger) because of a tweet was brilliant as it delighted customers while giving KLM enormous amounts of press. More details about the promotion can be found here. http://youtu.be/pqHWAE8GDEk or Google "KLM Twitter Surprise".

According to Twitter[38], here are the best practices for using the platform:

"Build your following, reputation, and customer's trust with these simple practices:

1. **Share.** *Share photos and behind the scenes info about your business. Even better, give a glimpse of developing projects and events. Users come to Twitter to get and share the latest, so give it to them.*
2. **Listen.** *Regularly monitor the comments about your company, brand, and products.*
3. **Ask.** *Ask questions of your followers to glean valuable insights and show that you are listening.*
4. **Respond.** *Respond to compliments and feedback in real time*
5. **Reward.** *Tweet updates about special offers, discounts and time-sensitive deals.*
6. **Demonstrate wider leadership and know-how.** *Reference articles and links about the bigger picture as it relates to your business.*

---

[38] https://business.twitter.com/basics/best-practices/

7. *Champion your stakeholders.* *Retweet and reply publicly to great tweets posted by your followers and customers.*
8. *Establish the right voice.* *Twitter users tend to prefer a direct, genuine, and of course, a likable tone from your business, but think about your voice as you Tweet. How do you want your business to appear to the Twitter community?"*

LinkedIn

LinkedIn is a great tool for connecting with business-to-business customers. I recommend participating in the LinkedIn groups your customers and influencers belong to so you can see what issues they are having, as well as to assist with questions that they may have. You will establish yourself as an expert and you can develop and nurture relationships.

I am involved in many LinkedIn groups for travel, tourism, restaurants, sales and marketing. Some of the groups that I participate in are for the purpose of understanding my prospects and assisting when I can, as well as to show thought-leadership and my expertise. Other groups that I participate in include my peers in incentives, events and meetings. Within these groups I try to add value, while I also ask for help when necessary. Overall, LinkedIn provides a great opportunity to network and problem solve.

LinkedIn is also great for connecting with people through a Direct Message (DM), although I am seeing more spam in my inbox this year compared to last.

YouTube

Video works wonders for converting website visitors to buying customers. The beauty with video is that it does not have to be polished like a television show. Taking a video with a flip camera or your smart phone is acceptable, assuming the lighting is good and the person holding the camera is not shaking. Show off your restaurant, destination, tour, resort, events or golf course. Why not have a video with "insider tips" or "insider information"? Perhaps you could say "Welcome to our kitchen, here is how we make the duck à l'orange" or "If you are teeing off on this hole, hit between 100 and 120 yards and aim to the right of the sand trap to avoid the trees as you dogleg left" or "Come with me and I will show you how you can get to the best kept secret in Whistler" etc.

You can also use video for PR purposes; to introduce yourself and show-off your business; to highlight your creative abilities if you are a DMC or a meeting planner; to train travel agents and meeting planners how to sell your property, destination or tour; and finally to explain your processes; for customer service. As a travel agent, you could post videos of your trips or site inspections to share with your clients and prospects.

The video itself can be footage that you shoot, a slide-show with music, a slide-show with a voice over or a person sitting in front of a web cam. The best part about video is that you can embed it on your website, show it on your Facebook page, pin it to Pinterest and, if it strikes a chord with viewers, you may just find that it gets plenty of shares.

After you take your video you need to upload it to the web. You can upload it to your website directly or you can upload it to YouTube (or one of the other video sharing sites). There have been horror stories of people losing all the videos they have uploaded to YouTube because they violated the terms of service, I still recommend posting to YouTube because of the Google ranking benefits. Make sure you are clear about the terms of service on sites where you post digital images. Guerrilla marketers always keep a back-up of their videos. Never rely on a third party service as your only source for storing your digital files. Do not be shy, grab that video camera and start showing the world everything they are missing because they have not become your customer yet.

Conclusion

In this chapter I highlighted some of the more popular social networking websites. If you have not yet ventured into social media I recommend that you do. Remember – your customers are already there and they are trying to engage with you. My recommendation is to approach social media in two ways: establish a presence and manage your brand. Establish a presence means that you create an account and you use that account consistently to be helpful, to engage with your customers and prospects, and to post occasional promotional messages. People know that this is where you are active and where they can communicate with both you and other customers. Manage your brand means that you track the mentions of your brand either manually or using a social media monitoring tool. You claim and optimize your accounts at these websites and you consistently respond to questions and reviews. Your presence at these websites is not as involved and it is reactive. The difference between the two approaches is like the difference between hosting an event versus answering the phone to respond to a query or complaint.

Review each of the social networking websites, including review and check-in websites as explained in the chapter about managing your online reputation. Spend time understanding where your customers are. It may be one of the "big three" – Facebook, Twitter and LinkedIn but do not limit yourself to those sites. Your customers may be using MySpace, a niche social networking site, or they may be connecting online to meet in person using a website like Meetup.com. After you choose which social networking sites to establish a presence, communicate to your customers and prospects that this is where they can find you by putting social media icons on your website and by listing your account names on print materials, for example http://facebook.com/marqueemarketing.

Guerrilla marketing tip: always think about building your email list – even on social media websites because you can build-up a huge following that will disappear if the website owner terminates your account.

Chapter 11 - Mobile Marketing

"I love the freedom of movement that my phone gives me. That has definitely transformed my life"

Sir Richard Branson

With the explosive growth of smart phones like iPhones, Android Phones and Blackberries, the move to searching for everything online is going to happen faster. If you are not reaching your customers (and potential customers) in the places they are searching for information, you are going to get left behind by your competition that is.

Why Mobile Matters

- 90 percent of searchers perform some offline follow up with businesses they find online such as calling for more information or making a purchase (source: comscore).
- 59 percent of local information seekers visit a business after looking up information about it on their cell phones (source: Google Mobile Insights).
- 51 percent of people would characterize their shopping behavior as research online, buy offline (source: NPD Group).
- 61 percent of online local searches result in an offline purchase (source: TMP/ comScore).
- 88.2 million US adults have redeemed an online coupon either online or offline (source: eMarketer).
- 39 percent of search engine users surveyed indicated that they "routinely felt frustrated" by not being able to find a local business online (source: Webvisible-Nielsen, 2009).
- Only 27 percent of 1500 businesses surveyed actively optimized their website for local search (source: Marketing Sherpa).

Mobile Websites

Many companies have no "mobile" version of their website, which makes it likely that someone searching for information on their phone will simply leave the page and look for another website that is mobile friendly. People will not want to stretch and tap their mobile screens to find the tidbit of information that they are looking for. If your website takes too long to load, you will simply be bypassed.

Many times, people who are searching for local businesses are looking for one of two things – a phone number or an address. They do not want to read the website or anything else; they are just trying to either call or get to the right location. Be sure your phone number and address are easily found and that the person can tap to call without doing anything else. If you operate a restaurant, people are likely looking for your menu and hours of operation too, so be sure to include them. Put yourself in the shoes of your customers and consider what they might be looking for while searching with a mobile phone and then create a separate mobile optimized website.

The statistics about people searching online and following up offline are too significant to ignore. As an example, if your target market consists of meeting planners, you will know that they are frequently out of their office. Planners may be researching for what you sell while commuting or on-site. Think about people stuck on the public transit in the middle of winter desperate to book that sunny getaway. While they likely will not book their entire trip on the phone, they will spend time searching travel sites for destination and resort information. Depending on what they find and how much planning is complete, they may even go so far as to tap to phone you to inquire or make a reservation. However, this may also just be an initial contact while waiting to arrive at a more secure location.

The good news is that mobile websites are very simple compared to full websites. Check out how simple the Olive Garden, Hyatt Regency Cancun and Fairmont's mobile websites are and contrast them with the Sandals website. You can check to see how your website looks on a mobile device by going to http://www.howtogomo.com

Examples of good mobile websites

Example of website not optimized for, or created for, mobile devices

Mobile websites are a necessity but there is one more incredibly powerful aspect of mobile marketing that is still underused – text messaging.

Text Messaging

Text messaging, or Short Messaging Service (SMS), has experienced huge growth in the number of people who use it regularly. And it is not only younger people who are using it - it is becoming more and more common with older users as well.

There are two huge advantages to text messaging that really cannot be matched by any other method of communication:

1. The majority of people have their phones with them virtually all the time, so those messages will reach them no matter where they are. People even sleep with their phones because they use the alarm feature to wake.
2. The vast majority of text messages get read almost instantly when they are received. Compare that to email that may go unopened for several days.

If your business is slow on a particular day, you could send a text message and reasonably expect to see results that same day. There's just no other advertising medium that is virtually guaranteed to be seen immediately.

Does that mean you need to be feverishly tapping out individual text messages to all your customers every time you want to send something? Not at all. There are services that will broadcast a text message to everyone who has requested to receive them from you. These services let you choose a regular phone number, called a Long Code, or a five digit number, called a Short Code, to use as your point of contact. Your customers just have to send a text to that number to sign up to receive text messages from you whenever you broadcast something out.

You can even set up an automatic response from these short codes, giving you the ability to offer an incentive to get people to opt into receiving those messages. For example, a restaurant might offer a coupon for a free appetizer on their next visit by texting the word "appy" to their short code number. When the customer sends the text, they get a response almost instantly with the details of how to get the free appetizer which could be as simple as "Show this message to your server on your next visit to claim your free appetizer."

QR Codes

A QR code is a 2D, quick response bar code that, when scanned with a mobile phone, does a specified action. The beauty of using a QR code in your marketing is that they are free to create.

QR Codes Can be Used to:

- Link to a mobile business card;
- Take you to a poll, sweepstakes or a contest;
- Take you to your Facebook Fan page;
- Replace traditional airline boarding cards;
- Redirect you to more information about the product or customer reviews of the product (when placed on a product or display);
- Redirect you to a mobile website which features a restaurant's menu;
- Pre-fill a Tweet;
- Take you to a squeeze page to sign up for a newsletter, demo, free trial;
- Replace a "my name is" name tag at a networking event;
- Reveal a recipe from a restaurant menu;
- Direct people to more information when added to a press release;
- Get a restaurant reservation (using OpenTable.com);
- Order food and beverages at a baseball game; and
- Deliver a coupon or value-add service for next purchase.

QR codes have been placed on the side of buildings, on billboards, on business cards, on T-shirts, on promotional products (such as a mug), in newspapers and magazines and on the side of a bus. They can be placed nearly anywhere, except radio.

The downside with using a QR code is that there are many people that do not have a smart phone or they do not know what to do when they see a QR code, so education is needed.

Mobile Apps

A mobile app is software with customized content that is downloaded onto a smart phone or tablet for a specific purpose. There are mobile apps for calendars, scanning QR codes, mobile payments, accessing Facebook and many other general, productivity or entertainment purposes. It is possible to have an app for your business, as long as it provides value to the person downloading it and it is approved by Apple and Google to be included in their app stores.

Mobile apps and mobile websites can be very similar, however there is a primary difference namely that a mobile website is accessible via an internet connection and a browser, whereas the mobile app is downloaded and stored on the phone. Some components of a mobile app could require that the app connect to the internet, perhaps to pull content from a database while other features may require the use of the GPS function of the device for displaying content.

Consider This

You are responsible for marketing a specific destination, either as a DMC or DMO. You have a number of target markets such as destination wedding brides; wedding planners; meeting planners; incentive travel planners; families; affinity groups etc. You can have one mobile app for all targets that highlights your destination, features partner properties, offers an opportunity to connect with you on social networking sites, permits posts to your wall and the upload of images and offers coupons, push notifications and so much more. That one app does many things and should be deemed valuable to your target markets.

Alternatively, you could have one app for weddings, for families, for affinity groups, for attendees of meetings and conferences and another for your channel partners. Granted most of the information that would be included in a mobile app is available on the internet but what you are doing is filtering the information and providing recommendations. People are inundated with information and an app filters the mass of it so problems can be solved quickly.

The downside of an app is that it does cost more to create than a mobile website and updates need to be downloaded to the app itself. However, the push notification ability is appealing, when the list of users is larger as long as you remember to use it for relevant, timely messages only.

As an aside, the debate between which is best (a mobile website or a mobile app) continues, so with everything else that you do, figure out what your objectives are and do some market research with your customers first.

Chapter 12 – Promotion Strategies

"There are no magic wands, no hidden tricks and no secret handshakes that can bring you immediate success but with time, energy and dedication you can get there"

Darren Rowse

What is the purpose of your promotion? Do you want to increase revenue, to increase exposure or to increase traffic? Not all of your promotions will be designed to increase profits and, with social media in particular, you should not be posting "me me me" posts all the time. Some of your promotions will be designed to increase exposure; after all, the majority of people that see your push marketing campaigns are not likely in the market to buy what you are selling today. You will want to stay at the forefront, so when they are ready to buy, they think of you.

Other promotions will be designed to increase targeted traffic to your website/blog, Facebook page, Pinterest account and to your physical business. The important consideration is to know what your objectives are before you start to plan your promotions.

The real value of using mobile, local and social media marketing is when you use them together, either in conjunction with traditional advertising methods or exclusively. If you place a print ad, or you have a radio ad, or TV ad, be sure to include a CTA that will result in adding a name and email or name and mobile phone number to your list. When you combine the list building strategy with the traditional advertising you will determine what compels people to act.

Promotional Strategies for Increasing Profit Right Now

In this section I explain promotions, coupons, BOGO and discounting. If you have a popular, successful business or if you are in the luxury sector, discounting and couponing is neither necessary nor wise. I also caution against discounting, if providing more value is possible. Instead of discounting by 25 percent, why not add value by 25 percent as it will cost you less? In the incentives chapter I explain strategies to increase profits by using sales incentives, employee recognition and loyalty programs. Those programs require more planning and a longer commitment and they are administered over a longer period of time.

The following promotions ideas are meant for actionable sales today or this week:

SMS Messaging

For driving sales today, guerrillas know there is no other method that is as effective as a mobile SMS blast to your list.

- A pizza restaurant segmented its opt-in list to neighborhoods and even large apartment buildings. They send a SMS blast to a specific neighborhood or apartment building with a promotion that is valid only for about an hour so that they can have one or two drivers delivering a whole bunch of pizzas to the same area at once. It is brilliant as they get more sales, more deliveries and spend less on labour and fuel all at the same time;
- If you own a restaurant and it is a Tuesday, which is a slow evening for you, send out a blast between 4 and 5 P.M. to invite your opt-in list to join you for "fill in the blank";
- If you have a decent lunch crowd with room for more then send a SMS promotion about 11:45 A.M. to offer a promotion valid until 2 P.M. that day. It should be more than just a reminder about the lunch special... offer a value-added incentive or a promotion that will get people to act immediately; and
- If you have a radio remote for an instore promotion, use the opportunity to capture emails and mobile phone numbers while giving something of value to drive sales today and in the future.

Email Marketing

Email marketing is also useful for filling empty seats/beds but with the open rate being as low as it is, I am not recommending it for last minute promotions, unless your audience is used to being surprised by a flash sale or unless you also include a social media and/or mobile marketing component.

Twitter

Twitter is very useful for some businesses who tweet often and tweet value. There are some mobile food vendors that tweet their location and almost immediately their raving fans are lining up. If your followers are actively engaged with your business Twitter can be useful to drive sales immediately.

Promotional Strategies for Increasing Exposure

Press releases

Press releases have evolved as a marketing tool. Years ago releases were used to gain exposure through traditional media such as TV, radio, newspapers and magazines. Guerrilla marketers know that press releases can be successfully used for an entirely new strategy. You still have to have a newsworthy announcement but when you submit your press release to an online distribution website, you also benefit from back links to your website, which are great for driving traffic to your website which, in turn, has a positive effect on your SEO.

Press releases are an effective way to get exposure, for numerous reasons. When you send out a press release, using an online distributions site such as PRweb.com, the release will be listed on many news websites within a few hours as well as having a reach far greater than you would have by sending individual press releases to specific editors or reporters. Many local publications are desperate for stories about businesses and people in their community, so you may be asked to provide further information for a newsworthy story.

The best strategy for press releases is to:

- Integrate your keyword phrase into the headline, sub-heading and lead sentence;
- Match your headline to the content of the press release;
- Keep your headline needs to be specific and concise;
- Hyperlink the keyword phrase in your first paragraph to a relevant page on your website or blog;
- Use the "About" section / boilerplate for more keywords and another link back to your website;
- Post your press release on the "news" area of your website (great for search engines, for journalists and potential partners/customers/employees). Remember the tips provided in the blog post section about the title, meta description and featured image as it applies here too; and
- Post your press release on Facebook, Google+, Twitter and to appropriate groups on LinkedIn.

Article Distribution

Article distribution used to be one of the favorite ways of SEO companies to obtain back-links for their clients. When you write an article for syndication you are doing so for the same reasons you write blog posts: to show thought leadership, expertise and to highlight products and services of value to the readers.

The goal of article syndication is to put your content in front of the readers and subscribers of other people's websites, prompting people to click through to your website for more information. Ironically, you are not writing for Google but Google will love you because you are providing the value that it wants for its customers (those who use the search engine).

The bio section of your articles needs to contain links back to the website or blog of the author, providing a way to drive traffic to your website.

Google Authorship

Google Authorship (http://authorlinks.net) is a new service launched by Google, where you can pay popular authors to write about and link to your website. It's an interesting concept and could be a valuable addition to your guerrilla marketing toolbox, especially if you do not already have a following of powerful influencers. "Author Links is a marketplace for the buying and selling of contextual links that appear in content ... As a web site owner, you're always looking for new places to get the word out about your products or services. By connecting with authors that are well-known in their industry or topic, you will get more visibility, you will get links directly to your web site, and will target the right visitors: your potential customers."

Guest Blog Posts

Huffington Post, Social Media Examiner and a number of other blogs rely on guest bloggers for their content. Readers love to hear from the experts, while the blog enjoys the free content provider by the guest blogger who, in turn, earns street credibility with this new audience. If you are interested in guest blogging just do a Google search for "guest blogging" or "guest blogging opportunities" and tourism, travel, restaurants, golf courses, travel agents or whatever your specialty is. The back-links, the comments and the exposure are wonderful for your business and, hopefully, sales.

Become an Author

Writing a book such as this is a time consuming process but when you leverage your book to elevate yourself above your competition, there really is no better way to gain exposure and credibility. If you do not have months or years to spend writing a 250+ page book yet you want to position yourself as an authority, an expert and/or a celebrity in your industry, niche or destination, you will be happy to hear that you can write, publish and market your book in less than one month – and after this book is published, I am going to do just that.

If you would like to learn how to write, market and leverage your book in this manner, please contact me at carol@carolwain.com to find out about my coaching, training, workshops and book creation, publishing and support services.

Photosharing

Images are another type of content that can help you extend your reach and get your company in front of potential customers. There are many different photosharing sites where you can post your pictures. Here are some of the more popular:

- Pinterest;
- Flickr.com;
- Photobucket.com;
- Imageshack.com;
- Imgur.com; and
- Picasa.com.

Posting images builds brand recognition. If people are searching online for what you offer and your company name or logo comes up in the search results, that will help to brand you in their mind. When they see your website listed in the search results, or find your Google+ Local listing on their smart phone the next time they go searching, they are going to recognize you over other companies that they have not heard of. If you have pictures of your office or place of business online, it is going to make it easier for them to recognize your business. (Remember to watermark your images.)

Promotional Strategies for Increasing Traffic

Traffic, for the sake of traffic is not the ultimate goal. Instead you want targeted traffic – traffic that represents your ideal customers. If you blog about a controversial topic or a current trend you may attract people interested in that topic but not how it relates to your business. You may hold a contest or sweepstakes that offers the latest iPhone as the prize and it may generate a list with thousands of entrants – but are they potential customers or worthless names that are only interested in the prize? I would rather have 100 ideal customers enter my sweepstakes, read my blog or come to my location than 10,000 untargeted people.

In the next chapter you will be introduced to fusion marketing, which is an underutilized business tool that can drive lots of targeted traffic – and sales – to your business. Some other examples of ways you can drive good traffic are:

- Writing a high-quality article in a popular magazine or blog that directs people to your website to sign-up for more information;
- Posting an update on social media about an upcoming event (with a CTA to go to your website for more information);
- Hosting a webinar that provides answers to the top 10 challenges your ideal customer has and then use social media and paid advertising to drive registration;
- Sending a text message blast about a short-term promotion;
- Inviting registered tradeshow attendees to visit your booth with a teaser that hints of an element of fun, exclusivity or chance; and
- Hosting an "invite only" event at your business – you invite your customers and give them the ability to invite 3 of their friends. Make it exclusive, fun and remarkable.

Conclusion

Guerrilla marketers do not rely on one type of promotional strategy – instead they use a combination of weapons and campaigns, which they test to determine effectiveness. Which strategies could you use to increase exposure, traffic or profits?

Part Three –
Leveraging Relationships

In this section we explore ways to leverage your relationships and encourage your employees, customers, prospects, vendors, partners and network to increase your profit.

Chapter 13 - Fusion Marketing

You need to be aware of what others are doing, applaud their efforts, acknowledge their successes, and encourage them in their pursuits. When we all help one another, everybody wins."

Jim Stovall

Fusion Marketing is a powerful, yet underused, guerrilla marketing weapon that is perfect for tourism. Fusion Marketing is any form of marketing where you leverage resources of another business to generate results far greater and with less effort and less cost than you could do by yourself. You also share risk and rewards.

Joint Ventures[39]

Here are two definitions of a Joint Venture (JV) and it is important to clarify which type of arrangement is being proposed by the parties early-on.

- A legal structure when two or more parties form a separate company for the purposes of creating a new product using the resources and expertise of the parties; and
- Collaboration between two or more parties to market a product (a marketing JV)

Marketing JVs are commonly used to expand into a new market. For example, Tourism New Zealand, Malaysia Airlines and Auckland International Airport combined efforts[40] to bring luxury-seeking visitors from India to New Zealand during monsoon season in India

For the purposes of this book, I will not be exploring the legal aspect of a JV and I encourage readers to check with their legal counsel before embarking on any type of contractual relationship.

Host / Beneficiary relationship

Host / Beneficiary [41] is a term coined by Jay Abraham and it is a type of marketing JV.

---

[39] http://www.inc.com/encyclopedia/joint-ventures.html
[40] http://www.tourismnewzealand.com/markets-and-stats/south-east-asia/india/marketing-activity/new-joint-venture-in-india-drives-high-end-travellers/
[41] http://www.greatresults.com/abraham/hostbeneficiary.html

- A host / beneficiary relationship is where Company A (the host) agrees to let Company B (the beneficiary) deliver a sales message to people who are the customers of Company A;
- The relationship is contractual;
- Company A announces a great deal that they have "negotiated" for their customers and it endorses that product or service. This builds the goodwill bank that Company A has with its customers while their customers receive a valuable, exclusive offer;
- Company B formulated the deal before approaching Company A and convinced Company A about the benefits to its business and its customers, while alleviating any concerns it may have over quality, service levels, marketing message and protection of Company A's customer list;
- Host / beneficiary arrangements can be set up to include a financial transaction where Company B pays Company A per lead or per sale, although they do not require consideration, particularly if the offer is very attractive to the host and its customers.

Strategic Alliances[42]

Strategic Alliances are fusion marketing relationships where the parties are not necessarily working with a common plan, but still benefit from each other's efforts

- The relationship is often informal;
- The parties come together for a particular purpose and then implement the strategy together;
- Deals could be as simple as sharing a booth at a trade show; creating an exclusive offer; using under-utilized resources of the other party; or partnering to combine buying power to reduce costs.

For example, a strategic alliance between a restaurant, hair salon, clothing store and a photographer for the purposes of hosting a "girl's night out" event could result in new business for each business.

---

[42] http://www.inc.com/magazine/20100601/how-to-build-business-alliances.html

JV Broker

A JV Broker is a person who connects businesses for the purposes of entering into fusion marketing agreements. The JV broker role is to find a distribution channel for a product or service and to connect the channel to the creator in a similar manner as a mortgage broker connects a bank to a potential homeowner.

Sohail Khan, http://sohail-khan.com/, one of the world's top JV experts, explained how JVs work in an interview (which can be found at http://carolwain.com). Some excerpts follow:

> *"Wal-Mart is a place where, when you go inside, they provide you with everything that you need; so it is very similar to a joint venture. They have a distribution which is the people, the foot floor traffic, and they are just going out there finding joint venture partners who have products that they can sell to their existing customers. That is a classic example a joint venture in play."*

> *"The biggest focus on joint ventures is about relationships. If you build relationships, joint ventures become easy because what happens is it does not become a proposal any more. It just becomes a request."*

> *"Make sure that any joint ventures you are doing are targeted. There is no point in building relationships or doing joint ventures with someone who has a 500,000 list that is not even remotely interested in your product or service."*

> *"I have a friend, his name is Captain Lou, and he does themed cruises. What he does is he goes into an industry and he becomes friends and builds a relationship with the influencers in the industry. He began with Mike Filsaime, the internet marketer. Mike Filsaime is the influencer and can bring the people. They have a cruise where over 500 people come on a ship every year to mastermind about internet marketing. He does another one for science fiction where he has gone to an influencer in that industry and he has got another one in the dating niche as well where he has gone to an influencer there and he said, 'Hey, you know what, I have access to these cruise ships. I get good deals. Would you like to head or represent a cruise under my banner and you bring the people, I will provide*

the cruise ship and the entertainment.' That is one of the biggest I have seen in the tourism industry, in terms of a friend, and they do multimillion dollars in revenue every year from that."

"Here is the thing I want to tell everyone about joint ventures. The secret of joint ventures is not to go out and find a product that you think can really sell and then find the market; it is finding the market first. Go and find the distribution or the market and then control the market, control the distribution and then go and find products to put into the marketplace. That is how you make millions of dollars doing joint ventures. You do not normally have people say that because not everyone wants everyone to know exactly how it is done, but that is the secret of joint ventures."

"I think the most common mistake when it comes to joint ventures is people not thinking about the win-win situation. Some people are just out for themselves and they just think about how they want to make money. They are too interested in their own product for example. They do not think of the benefits, or they do not think of what they should be giving, rather than receiving. One of my mottos in life is, "Give first, ask later." I always tend to go out there and give as much I can, provide people with as much as I can give and then it just becomes natural that someone will turn around and say to you, 'Okay, Sohail, so how can I help you?' I think the biggest mistake in joint ventures is not having a giving nature. A lot of people approach me or approach people I know for joint ventures, but it is like, 'Dude, first of all, I do not think you know what I do and it would be nice for you to find out more about me. The product that you are promoting is not right for my list of my customers.'"

"Nowadays what happens is some of these big companies, who do not understand how joint ventures work, see each other as competitors and that is where a third person, like myself, who is a joint venture broker, would come into the equation and basically help these companies get together and pull the partnership. My job is being wholly independent in the actual joint venture deal so I would only share information *between both companies that I was in effect told or allowed to share. I would manage the joint venture deal to make sure that both companies actively are doing what they are supposed to be doing in the joint venture deal."*

Fusion Marketing Examples:

Joint Venture

The owner of an evening walking tour in New Zealand, Adventure Puketi, entered into a joint venture marketing arrangement[43] with a restaurant, Food at Wharepuk, to offer a combined service called "Dining under the Stars" that also features a performance by a local kapa haka group.

In this instance, the combined products create a complete evening experience for the guest while the joint venture partners present a unique product that they jointly market to benefit all parties.

Host / Beneficiary Relationship

When I was a travel agent, I used to look for customers who drove luxury cars because that was one way I defined my ideal customer. If I had known about fusion marketing back then, I would have proposed a JV to a car dealership. The owner of a new upscale boutique[44] also identified her ideal client based on the cars they drove (BMWs) so she approached a dealership to offer a silk kimono to each female customer. The kimono sold for $100 but cost $16, so it was an appealing incentive. It was so appealing that 600 women redeemed the offer letter that the dealership sent them. The women had to pick-up their kimono at the store, and while at the store they also spent an average of $400 on other merchandise. For $9,600 ($16 x 600) the boutique owner got 600 new customers who spent on average $400, which is $240,000 in sales. That is a fantastic return on investment.

As a tourism business, you should be creating your own fusion partner network to offer products and services that will bring you new customers. An event venue can partner with a florist and a photographer for wedding prospects; a restaurant can partner with a

[43] http://www.forestwalks.com/forest-dining-experience/
[44] http://www.entrepreneur.com/article/185880

golf course; a ski resort can partner with a sporting goods store; a spa can partner with a hair salon; a travel agent can partner with a car dealership; a hotel can partner with a car service. The list goes on and on.

JP Maroney told me about a jeweler who added 4,137 customers in seven weeks by using a different type of campaign[45]. The jeweler (the beneficiary) sent an offer to all the members of his local Chamber of Commerce (the host). The promotion provided local business owners with a free, no-strings attached $50 gift certificate to give as a holiday gift to each employee and $100 gift certificate for the business owner. Owners would simply fill in a form with details to create the certificates and fax it back to him. The gift certificates were created to look like the employer actually purchased them for the employees.

At first the jeweler was concerned because he had opened himself up to an "unlimited" number of $50 certificates. However, the jeweler knew that his CLV is $2,400 and his Customer Acquisition Cost (CAC) -- the cost to attract and close a new customer, is $400, so at keystone markup (doubling the cost of an item to determine the retail cost), the worst case scenario was that it would cost him $25 ($50 divided by 2) per certificate redeemed.

The promotion started working within fifteen minutes of launch and cost him less than $90. The jeweler realized an increase in sales of 56 percent in the first three weeks; a 110 percent sales increase in monthly sales within ninety days; and he continues to market to the 4,137 people that redeemed the original gift certificate.

Hypothetical Example

An upscale restaurant seeks to have a big launch when it opens in 6 weeks. The ideal customer is a white collar professional, between the ages of 35 and 55 who drives a luxury car. The owner approaches a local luxury car dealership to offer them an opportunity to give their customers a free dinner consisting of an entrée, a glass of wine and a choice of either an appetizer or dessert during the first month the restaurant is open.

---

[45] http://freebyb.com/landing-page-1

The pitch is that the restaurant owner will do all the work, including writing the endorsement letter, and paying for stationery and postage. To sweeten the deal, the restaurant owner offers the car dealership principal an incentive – a team appreciation dinner for his staff within the first four weeks after opening, (with an advance reservation, subject to availability), which is attractive to the dealer principal because he can "treat" his team on someone else's tab.

The restaurant receives its ideal customers during the first few weeks in business and, with a solid plan to impress them during their visit and a follow-up plan to get them to return, the owner's marketing costs are reduced to postage, the cost of the food, beverages and labor.

Strategic Alliance

James Schramko, SuperFastBusiness.com, explained how he created a highly successful sales event using strategic alliances (go to http://carolwain.com for the interview)

> *"Going back to the (Mercedes-Benz) car dealership, it is a good example because it is a relevant lesson that I have been able to apply over and over again. At the time we had no marketing budget so I had to find innovative ways to acquire customers. I went out to the high-end music manufacturers, high-end wine companies and high-end banking and finance companies. I was able to access their database by holding an event in our showroom.*
>
> *I would actually have the wine company set up a stall and supply wine for an evening and invite their customers. I would have the top-level banking company invite their best customers, their private equity customers, into the Mercedes showroom for an evening of wine and art. I would have an art gallery supply art, which we put on the wall and they could sell and we would not take any commission, so they could display their best art and put it up on the wall. We had the Premium Sound from Bang & Olufsen with the music supplied by them. They would bring in their music equipment and also a live string quartet. We had the whole thing – the wine, the art, the music and the nice cars – but I was drawing from the customer base of non-compete industry databases.*

We got the best music customers, the best bank customers, the best art gallery customers and the best wine customers in our showroom. Of course, they all go into our database then because we have a promotion where they get to enter their details to win prizes. We draw for the prizes but then we get to keep the email and we can market to them next time."

Considerations

When creating a compelling offer to attract a fusion marketing partner, it is essential to factor in your three key numbers so that you can be sure the offer is a win-win-win for your business, your fusion marketing partner and for their customers.

1. Your CAC;
2. Your CLV; and
3. Your profit margin.

It can be a bit scary to look at an offer at face value, so it is important that you consider the CLV and profit margin too. If your CLV is high and your profit margin is high, then your initial offer can be more generous. Alternatively, if your CLV and/or your profit margin is low, a fusion marketing arrangement may not be the best marketing tool for you.

For example, if your average customer has a CLV of $3,000 and your ideal customer has a CLV of $6,000; you have a 20 percent profit margin and your CAC is $200. How much would you be willing to spend to attract more customers, in general, and more ideal customers, specifically? Doing some very simple math, the ideal customer currently nets you $6,000 x 20% = $1200 - $200 = $1,000 and your average customer nets you $3,000 x 20% = $600 - $200 = $400. It makes sense to enter into an arrangement where you reduce your CAC for your average customer since the CLV is only twice as much as the CAC. However, it makes more sense to enter into an arrangement to attract more ideal customers even if the CAC is higher than $200 since the ideal customer nets you 2½ times as much.

Caution

When choosing your fusion marketing partners, remember you both must share the same standards and values. Your reputation can be damaged by an unequal partnership. Also, choose fusion marketing partners that offer complementary products and services but do not

150

compete with you. Your fusion marketing partners need to understand win-win-win situations. If your partnership is not collaborative, the partnership will not work. Partners need to be fully committed to the arrangement and they need to see how it will benefit all parties. Finally, if you are the host, be sure that you maintain control of your own list; be sure to be choosy when entering relationships and always ask yourself "Will my customers appreciate this 'gift'?" If not, do not enter into the agreement, no matter how lucrative it may be for you as you do not want to upset your customers.

Action Steps

Put on your thinking cap and consider your customer and where else they might shop, then approach those business owners with a fusion marketing proposal. Remember, the proposal does not need to be complicated. You can say "Can you promote my business to your customers and I will promote your business to my customers for the next month?" or "I would like to give your customers _____, which will create goodwill for your business while it brings new customers to mine.

Chapter 14 – Customer Experience

"If you do build a great experience, customers tell each other about that. Word of mouth is very powerful."

Jeff Bezos

The experience your customer has is the result of all your decisions. It is your litmus test to determine if you have hired well, trained well, provided the right tools for your employees and provided the right environment for delivering exceptional experiences. After all, you cannot expect to "Wow" your customers if you have not kept up the maintenance on your property, or if you have cut back on staffing, or worse, if you cannot find and keep good quality employees.

On the flip side, an employer that invests should expect to see happier customers because she will receive consistent, positive experiences that deliver on the brand promise. Happy customers make the lives of the employees a whole lot easier, which in turn helps to create a desirable workplace.

In his book, The Thank You Economy[46], Gary Vaynerchuk talks about the Joie de Vivre hotels in California. As part of their Dream Maker program, the hotels ask each guest to provide a significant amount of personal information upon registration so that they can find ways to give their guests a memorable experience. This program challenges the employees to come up with ways to provide exceptional guest service. Gary tells a story about a reservations manager, Jennifer Kemper, at the Hotel Durant in Berkeley, which incidentally is the number three hotel in Berkeley according to TripAdvisor. One of the hotel guests needed multiple, long-term stays because her son, a 20 year old Berkeley student, was undergoing chemotherapy treatment while trying to continue with his studies. The guest needed to visit often to help her son during his sessions but some of the dates that she needed were not available. Jennifer told her guest that she would be taken care of but she did not stop there. Jennifer thought of the guest's plight and determined that she would be a great candidate for the Dream Maker program. A few days later, Jennifer went and bought a card, sunflowers, chamomile tea and a dragonfly mug with a built-in strainer. The card said "For a loving mother who deserves to

---

[46] http://thankyoueconomybook.com/

relax. Your family is in our thoughts and prayers." Naturally, this touched the heart of the guest, who continued to stay at that property until her son graduated. This example of a fantastic customer experience also shows how a simple touch can have a viral effect. Imagine how many people heard about this story from the guest and her son. That caring, attentive service, which is one of the guerrilla marketing principles, provided exposure to this hotel they could never afford through traditional marketing. Talk about a win-win situation.

I had an equally impressive experience on a fam trip hosted by the Orlando CVB. During the registration process, I was asked some personal questions about the charities I support. Imagine my surprise and delight when I came back to my room one evening and I discovered a note that said that Orlando CVB donated money (in my name) to a favorite charity. What a great gesture that was not only personal and unique but also touched my heart.

Contrast this to multiple poor experiences on the same cruise line, which I have vowed never to travel with again. For instance, I was out-and-out-lied-to about an upgrade I had been promised as well as being assigned a cabin that had been occupied by another passenger to perhaps worst of all hearing a family member publicly disrespected. All of these experiences were caused by the employees' poor judgment in dealing with a customer, which should have been addressed during orientation and training. The true test was when I wrote to the customer care center, outlining detail after detail of my poor experience and I received a template response. In the end this was a wasted opportunity to address an unhappy customer experience and make it right but it does demonstrate quite emphatically, the decision makers of this cruise line do not care about customer service.

The online reviews for this cruise line cite more complaints about poor service, poor quality and misrepresentations – this floating resort is steering itself into rough waters.

It is corporate suicide to deliver an experience contrary to your brand promise.

Delivering Exceptional Customer Experiences

In earlier chapters I defined your ideal customer and your value differentiators to help you to create a profitable business that attracts the type of customers you are best suited to serve exceptionally well. These exercises help you to create your own "Blue Ocean Strategy", to create your brand promise and to help you to speak directly to those you wish to serve.

These next steps are to ensure that you have the pieces in place to deliver on your brand promise so that your ideal customers become brand advocates.

Here are some broad stroke suggestions to deliver exceptional experiences:

- Review your employees;
    - o Who is capable of delivering exceptional service each and every time?
    - o Who needs some coaching / training?
    - o Who needs to move on to a job better suited to his skills and attitude?
- What policies, processes and rules need to be adjusted to make the experience easier to deliver?
- What changes do you need to make to your physical location, products and services offered?
- What changes should you make to your marketing to attract your ideal customer?
- What can you do to "Wow" people? You need many ways so that customers are pleasantly surprised each time;
- Empower your employees to take ownership of a customer and his needs;
- Be honest. If you cannot fulfill requests say so. Managing expectations is an important part of the customer experience;
- Keep your promises. Along the same lines of being honest. If you say you are going to do it, do it;
- Every employee in your organization needs to know how their role impacts the experience of their customers. Tell them why their performance is important. It is not just the front-line customer service reps or sales people that impact the experience it is everyone... from the front line staff to the janitor to the executives to the back-office staff. Each person makes an impact in one way or another;
- From formal surveys, to informal requests that ask "How can we do better?" to requests for written reviews and

testimonials, you need to know how you are doing in the eyes of your customers, so ask and measure against your standard of excellence;

- Ask your employees to tell you what bottlenecks and roadblocks are lowering their productivity and customer satisfaction. Then fix them;
- There are customers who are high-maintenance and outrageously demanding. Those customers may have a nugget or two of insight into how you can improve (as you figure out how to fire them). It is the quiet customers that need to be asked their thoughts as they are potentially the most dangerous to your business success. Many people would rather just stop doing business with you than complain. You need to find ways to connect with them in a non-confrontational way to find out what they think about how you can improve;
- Make employees accountable. Their performance bonuses, incentive plans and recognition programs need to have a component related to the customer experience. For front-end employees this could be based on those surveys, reviews, testimonials and "tell us what you think" questionnaires. For back-end employees it could be based on components that they directly impact. Are the comments on the quality of your brand?
- Embrace social media. Your customers are going to talk about you anyway, so be part of the conversation;
- Develop a personal relationship with your clients/customers. As a customer, I love it when I am recognized when I walk in the store or at the checkout. My favorite grocery store has a cashier that has called me by name for years. For B2B customers, spend time getting to know your customers, prospects and influencers in the most natural way you can;
- Anticipate your customer's needs;
- Apologize. No matter how hard you try, some days are just not great. If something goes wrong, take ownership, apologize and make it right. It will greatly improve your customer experience because most people accept that things go wrong occasionally (especially when you usually do things well);

- Invest in training. Your staff must be more knowledgeable about your products and services than your customers; and
- Thank customers for their business in a genuine manner.

On the one hand, delivering exceptional customer experiences sounds easy… just follow these steps. In reality it is hard to do because each and every touch point and it requires constant vigilance because it is those experiences that your customers talk about when they talk about your business with friends and family and when they rant about in an online review. Monitor constantly and fix problems promptly. Your cash flow, profit, employees and customers will all be more positive.

100,000 members and counting

I had the opportunity to talk with Dave Smith, Founder and General Manager of Spice UK, which is an adventure sports and leisure membership group in the UK founded 31 years ago. Dave and his team have grown the business to include multiple franchises that have catered to over 100,000 members over the years. I asked him how he has grown his customer base.

> *"Well, it is all word of mouth for us. Over the years, we have been involved in all sorts of advertising and various ways of trying to get the word out there but what works for us is word of mouth. It is a difficult concept to get across very quickly in an ad in a newspaper or a radio and what we found, over many years, is that when we analyze how people have come to join, 95 percent to 98 percent of them have joined because their friend is in it and they have heard what their friends are doing and they want a bit of that. So we got into the word of mouth advertising skill set. There are things that you can do to help generate word of mouth, and that is quite obvious really, quite simple, which is to really over deliver and really wow your members so that they are thrilled about what they are doing and go back to work on Monday full of stories and full of praise and share it with their friends and family. So, to be honest, that is where our energy lies.*
>
> *Now, the thing that is changed in the past five years, is word of mouth has gone electronic, as you know, with social networking, so we have harnessed the social networks because*

that is all that is, really, is not it? It is word of mouth. It is just happening electronically and through everybody's mobiles and computers now."

When asked specifically what the Spice leaders do to add to their customer experience, Dave responded, *"We over deliver, we might say, 'oh, we bought wine for everybody tonight', or we might buy everybody a drink when they come in. Some of that may be cost may have been factored into to the ticket price but it is a decision by the coordinators, to think of ways to over deliver. It is good business to do that. You can obviously cut your margin to do it if you did not plan for the surprise but you get the extra wow factor which is important.*

We text people before events or after events just to say things like 'Oh, you are going to have a great time tonight. Don't forget to bring your camera.'

We put the online chat facility onto our website and we are finding people are on there in the evening and they want to chat. They want to ask a question about the club and these people might be members who are looking at booking an event and they are not sure about something; or they might be people who are thinking about joining. When you answer people at 9:00 o'clock and 10:00 o'clock at night, they are really impressed and it really is a good connection. They are saying to us 'wow, you are really there'.

We try to deliver a really high level of service and provide a very personal service to people. We really make an effort. It is little things like, remembering people's names – and there's a couple of techniques that we use for that – and then we use their names, we remember what they did with us last time and reference that so we make it very, very personal with a lot of little things."

Spice could not have grown without providing a consistent experience that people want to share with their friends and family. How can you use your great reputation to grow your own business?

Chapter 15 – Customer Engagement and Community Building

"If you work just for money, you will never make it, but if you love what you are doing and you always put the customer first, success will be yours."
Ray Kroc

Perhaps the easiest way to define "engagement" is with a story of two couples who met at Montego Bay Airport in 1995 – Dave and Catherine and my fiancé, Steve and I. Both couples were to be married at the same Sandals resort one day apart. We all became fast friends on the transfer bus between the airport and the resort and we chose to attend each other's wedding. We had a fantastic time and were completely satisfied with our weddings and our vacation / honeymoon. We have kept in touch over the years and each time we get together, we talk travel.

Dave and Catherine have returned to Sandals once or twice a year every year since. They have vacationed at the majority of Sandals properties and they have their favorite properties and their favorite rooms. They have earned multiple pairs of sandals, along with a one week stay. Catherine talks of ways they are pampered, she tells of the relationships she has with the staff and of special treatment they receive. Dave and Catherine are absolutely engaged with the brand and they are loyal customers. Catherine is an influencer, a brand advocate and so loyal that whenever I suggest another brand, she declines.

Steve and I have returned to Sandals once and we have stayed at their sister brand, Beaches, twice. We always have a fantastic time and we recommend the brand to our networks. We would be considered satisfied customers but we are not as loyal because we love to travel to different destinations and try different resorts each time. We are influencers and we advocate for the brand but we are not engaged because we are not emotionally invested. Does Sandals know who I am though? I do not think so. Do they know how influential Catherine is? I sure hope so. The smartest action that Sandals – and you – could take would be to take stock of past guests / customers and influencers and work hard to leverage those relationships.

Customer Engagement

When someone is engaged with your business, they have invested their heart in your business. Engagement is not the same as satisfaction – it is so much more because customers can be satisfied with their experience but they do not have any emotional connection to your business. Loyalty is not the same as engagement because your customer can be a loyal customer only for convenience and would most likely change if her circumstances change. Customer experience is not the same as engagement either because engagement goes beyond managing the touch points a customer has with your business. Instead engagement is personal with a positive ongoing relationship between the parties.

To create engagement with your customers, you need to have the basics in place:

- A good product that is unique from competitors;
- Exceptional, consistent service delivered by employees that care; and
- A way of interacting with your customers in a personal, yet scalable manner to nurture ongoing relationships.

You need a community.

Community Building

To build a community you need to identify a number of key people so that you know who to invite to join your community.

- Your current customers;
- Your prospects;
- Your ideal customers;
- Your influencers; and
- Your best employees for supporting a community.

The Role of Influencers

It is easy to identify your current customers, ideal customers and best employees. However, identifying your influencers – both positive and negative – is more challenging because there are public influencers and unknown influencers. The public influencers post positive comments on review sites, tell their friends about you on social networking and micro blogging sites, write testimonials and cover your good news in the media.

Just as there are people that publicly and positively influence your customers to buy from you there are also people that negatively influence your customers and prospects using those same channels and you can (and should) track both positive and negative sentiment using software such as Trakur.com or SocialMention.com. As part of your reputation management, you should acknowledge and thank the positive influencers, which will reinforce their assertions and their appreciation of your business. The public negative influencers need to be acknowledged too but the conversation should be private while you attempt to resolve their issues. Always remember though, that your private conversation may end up public, so be careful how you respond.

The challenge for marketers is not with public influencers, it is with unknown influencers. Past customers, disgruntled ex-employees and competitors influence your customers and the only sustainable way to ensure that you do not lose business because of their influence is to ensure that you treat all people well while your employees deliver exceptional experiences consistent with your brand promise. I have influenced more travel purchase decisions in the past few years than I ever did as a retail travel agent and I believe it is because people trust my judgment while knowing that I am not being compensated. I recently saw a post from a Facebook friend that vacationed at the same property my family had stayed at a month earlier (Signature at MGM). I was confused because I thought she stayed at a property near Red Rock Canyon, so I asked her a question on her Facebook wall. She responded:

> *"Actually Carol, your pics of the suites swayed my decision! We just decided to rent a car for one day as well and would have had to the whole time otherwise. Very nice condo, service and view. Liked the pools and cabanas too."*

As you are reviewing your business, pay attention to those who influence purchase decisions both positively and negatively. As an aside, if you are interested in learning more about media manipulation, the book Trust Me, I'm Lying by Ryan Holiday will open your eyes.

The Rise and Fall of Airwaves

In college we had a large group of friends who regularly socialized together. One weekend, my friend, Joyce convinced us to go to Airwaves, a biker bar. We went again the next weekend and before long this became our regular hangout. The owners adapted by hiring a DJ and making changes to accommodate their new free-spending customers. I recall we "owned" this club in our minds because the majority of the customers were from our core group of friends. It was a great experience for us and I believe the owners were thrilled too as we were spending a fortune there every weekend.

The owners were likely wondering what happened though when, all of a sudden, we stopped frequenting the place. The reality, of course, was that most of us graduated at the same time. Shortly thereafter the club closed. It is an important lesson to remember not only for knowing who your influencers are but also for understanding your customer mix and getting inside their heads so that you are not blind-sided by customer transitions.

Referrals

I have had clients with a lower than average CLV but a higher than average referral rate. I have had prospects refer me to their network. I received referrals from an incentive software company that was acquired and changed direction and needed a replacement solution for their customers. When I received a lead for a $50 million per year incentive program, I referred it to another incentive company because they could better support the client. Referrals are fantastic ways to increase your profits, so always ask your happy customers, your friends and family and your prospects for referrals.

Creating a Community around Your Local Business

Either alone or with other fusion marketing partners, you can build a community around your local business that caters to residents by creating fun, educational, experiential and/or inspiring events such as:

- Photo Contests;
- Customer Appreciation Events;
- Best tips for _____ webinars or seminars;
- Creating a "Passport to Savings" booklet;
- Funding a school or community charity;
- Holding a scavenger hunt; and

- Adopting a community.

I love the scavenger hunt concept because it engages the local community with your business in a fun way. Depending on your customers, you can use mobile marketing and have the participants scan QR codes to get taken to a website to pick up the clues or you can use a more traditional way of providing clues. You could even follow the lead of the television show "The Amazing Race" to engage participants in activities to receive their next clue. Either way, I recommend that the clues and/or the activities tie back to the sponsoring businesses and that there is some sort of award celebration at the end. This type of event is fun and gives people a reason to engage one-on-one with the business. It is also memorable and creative and costs very little for the benefit (and possible media coverage) that can result. It is a true guerrilla marketing tactic.

Tangelo Park Community

Harris Rosen, Founder and President of Rosen Hotels and Resorts, literally built a successful community in a neighborhood that connects his business to his employees and to the community. Many businesses have not enjoyed the success that Mr. Rosen has experienced and they are not able to contribute to the degree that he has. However, the concept of supporting your local community, to help them better their lives and to contribute to their health and well-being can be done by even the smallest tourism business.

> *"Twenty years ago while I was sitting at my desk I realized just how blessed I have been, well beyond anything that I would ever imagined. I felt very strongly that I needed to demonstrate my gratitude by giving back to those who need a helping hand. I always believed that education was the key to leveling the playing field. I wanted to create a foundation dedicated to education so I called a couple of friends of mine, both of whom had been in education most of their lives. Sarah Sprinkle, who is an early childhood education expert, and Bill Spoon, who spent most of his life as the principal at one of the largest high schools in central Florida and we met.*
>
> *Within a very short period of time, we put together what is now known as the Tangelo Park Program. The program consists of providing a free preschool education for every two, three and four-year-old in the Tangelo Park neighborhood. To*

accomplish this, we developed ten little preschools in the neighborhood with a maximum capacity of six children per school. In addition to preschool, we provide full scholarships for vocational school, community college or a four-year college in Florida. The Rosen Foundation pays for everything... We pay all expenses, to include tuition, books, travel, etc. The neighborhood has transformed itself (it was a poor neighborhood with high rates of crime) to one which has been recently referred to by the Sheriff of Orange County as "an oasis". Crime is down between 50-60 percent. High school graduation rates are at 100 percent; college admissions and graduation rate at an unheard of 77 percent. In fact when our kids start kindergarten, after being in school from two to four, they are tested, and 70 percent of them are tested as gifted, this is due primarily to the tremendous advantage they have of a preschool education. The ten little pre-schools are in the neighborhood, each accommodating six youngsters. They are for the most part located in private single family homes in the neighborhood. The caregivers are all certified care providers and we provide them with whatever supplies they need, be it books, computers, games, etc. This is a great template. Thus far, we have sent approximately 200 kids to college. From a neighborhood that was graduating about 50 percent from high school, we now graduate 100 percent.

In Florida, they have something called the F-CAT, the Florida Comprehensive Achievement Test, and Tangelo Park is one of two elementary schools located in a disadvantaged neighborhood that has been rated an A school. We have been an A school for six of the past seven years. Unbelievable success! Our dream is to encourage others to adopt low-income neighborhoods throughout the United States and to replicate our program."

For those of us who do not have twenty years of success, like Mr. Rosen, you can build your goodwill bank by contributing in your own way to your own neighborhoods. It helps the residents, it helps the community, it attracts employees, it attracts customers and it certainly feels good.

Creating a Community Around Your Business

Guerrillas know that businesses that sell to visitors and through channel partners can create a community online using social media:

- Facebook Page interaction;
- Facebook Groups;
- Facebook Contests;
- LinkedIn Groups;
- Twitter; and
- Pinterest.

They also hold webinars and tele-seminars or they post videos, podcasts, pictures and updates on their website with the "comments" function enabled.

Offline tourism community building uses the more traditional techniques such as:

- Private events at trade shows and conferences;
- Travelling road-show in conjunction with their DMO;
- Fam trips for travel agents, meeting planners, journalists, bloggers and other influencers;
- Sponsorships; and
- Contests and Sweepstakes.

The best approach is to start online to find and build your community. Engage with them online in the following ways:

- Contests;
- Polls;
- Questions that you ask and that you answer;
- Coupons;
- Advanced ticket or seat purchases; and
- Community-only promotions.

Move to more specific interaction with personalized, targeted emails (be sure they opt-in to each list) and stay connected to build relationships with offline communications such as phone calls, mailers and in-person meetings and events.

The stronger your community, the tighter the connections are between your members and your business. People want to be part of a tribe and, when you treat them with respect and consideration, they will support you and your business and they will become more engaged. When your community is engaged with you, you can collect more information and insight so that you can deepen your ongoing relationships with them, while you develop products and services your customers will really respond to. It truly is a win-win situation so focus on your community and your community will support you.

Chapter 16 – Guerrilla Employees

"You can dream, create, design, and build the most wonderful place in the world...but it takes people to make it a reality."

Walt Disney

Guerrilla employees increase your profit and engage your customers and they are your most valuable asset. Guerrilla employees are not easy to find by resume screening software or by manually reviewing resumes but they are easy to see when you are at other businesses or when you are walking through your own business. They are the people that show that they are excited about their work and they go above and beyond to be helpful. Customers love being served by these types of employees and they reward great service by buying more.

Guerrilla employees are employees who take control of their lives and their careers. They understand that they are responsible for their own happiness and their own successes and failures and it shows in their work. Guerrilla employees are engaged employees and engaged employees make your profits soar.

I am a huge fan of the television show "Undercover Boss" because the show always highlights problems that employees need to deal with on a regular basis because top level executives did not understand about what was going on at the customer and employee levels. Oftentimes, the show spotlights exceptional employees who make the most of the situation and come up with suggestions or implement solutions themselves. These employees are a fantastic asset to the company and they deserve the recognition they receive. It is unfortunate that it takes a television show to get feedback from the employees to the senior management and that without the show their efforts may not have been recognized.

This happens far too often in business and it is my goal to draw attention to the opportunities that can be embraced when employers hire well, train well and communicate openly with their employees.

Dr. Frank Mulhern of Northwestern University and Don Schultz, Heidi Schultz and Robert Passikoff studied the link between employee behavior and spending at an international hotel chain and they concluded that *"Customer perceptions of the brand and the employee behaviors that influenced them had a direct and positive impact on how much money customers spend per visit over time."* In their report, *"Employee Behavior Increases Customer Spending"*[47] they found that when survey participants reported that employees "tried to satisfy" the needs of the customer, spending increased significantly. A 10 percent increase in effort resulted in a 22.7 percent increase in customer spending.

Guerrilla employees can be hard to find but they will be easy to retain if both your culture and your brand promises and delivers excellence. The key is to create a business that attracts and retains the great employees while weeding out those that are better suited elsewhere. Employee engagement, like customer engagement, is the emotional connection an employee has with your business. Engaged employees stay for what they can give, whereas disengaged employees stay for what they can get.

These Employee Engagement Statistics are Mind Boggling:

- The cost of disengagement in the US is estimated to be $370 billion due to absenteeism, productivity, accidents, theft and turnover. (source: Gallup)
- A comparison of Fortune's annual list of "100 Best Companies to Work For"[48] and the stock market shows that from 1998 – 2008, the "100 Best" have produced 4 times as much as the market in general. (source: Russell Investment Group)
- Organizations with employees who have "above average" attitudes towards their work had 38 percent higher customer satisfaction scores, 27 percent higher profits and 22 percent higher productivity. (source: Gallup)
- Companies that are raising engagement levels during the economic downturn are increasing revenue growth by 4½ times more than poor performing companies. (source: Hay Group)
- 70 percent of engaged employees indicate they have a good understanding of how to meet customer needs; only 17 percent of non-engaged employees say the same. (source: Wright Management)
- 78 percent of engaged employees would recommend their company's products of services, versus 13 percent of the disengaged. (source: Gallup)

---

[47] http://www.businessresultsthroughpeople.org/displaycommon.cfm?an=1&subarticlenbr=91
[48] http://www.greatplacetowork.com/our-approach/what-are-the-benefits-great-workplaces

- 86 percent of engaged employees say they very often feel happy at work, versus 11 percent of the disengaged. (source: Gallup)
- 59 percent of engaged employees say that their job brings out their most creative ideas against only 3 percent of disengaged employees. (source: Gallup)
- 18 percent of disengaged employees actually undermine their co-workers' success. (source: Gallup)
- 85 percent of a company's assets are related to intangible capital such as knowledge and human talent. (source: Brookings Institute)
- Employee turnover costs companies in the U.S. more than $140 billion annually in recruiting, training, replacement, administrative and other costs (source: Keep Employees Inc.)

I had the pleasure of speaking with David Zinger, who runs the Employee Engagement Network (http://employeeengagement.ning.com). David's background is in educational psychology and counseling psychology. He worked for approximately 17 years with Seagram as their employee assistance counselor and really got to know the workplace from the inside out, both at a personal level for employees and at an organizational level. I asked him for his definition of "employee engagement". David responded,

"In some fashion it just seems to be a buzz word and a fad. Lots of people hear about it and hear that it can increase profit and income, and help customers, and so they just want to get on some sort of bandwagon. At its worst it is a survey of employees' attitudes done about once every two years, and nothing much more happens. At its best I really think engagement is a connection. It is a connection to results, a connection to performance, a connection to each other, a connection to the organization and a connection to customers. Really to avoid the buzz word, I tend to often substitute the word 'connection' – strong robust connection. It goes both ways: from a manager to an employee and an employee to a manager, from the company to the employee, and the employee to the company."

I asked him "Why do you believe that so many companies are jumping on this bandwagon?" He replied,

> "Well, the financial numbers and the metrics are there. Back in 2002, Gallup estimated that a disengaged employee costs an organization about $3,400.00 for every $10,000.00 in salary. The day of just telling people to do things and expecting them to do it is no longer tenable. The day of saying, 'Well, I am paying you, so you better do it,' is not necessarily going to happen. I think in the early days for many organizations it was to get an edge. I think now it is just to stay abreast with everybody else in there. Really looking at those connections with employees and what is going on, and they recognize that everyone working in an organization, whether you are a CEO, a president or you are the new hire from yesterday, is an employee.

> There are really strong correlations between customer engagement and employee engagement. You start to see strong correlations between increased income and satisfaction levels with employee engagements. The person working is connected to their job, connected to everybody in the organization, connected to customers and you know it is going to make a difference."

> "Towers Perrin, the Hay Group, Mercer, Blessing White and Gallup, have all done massive global studies that show the business case. Over in the UK, David MacLeod has convened a task force that shows the time and impact of engagement in the entire UK and he wrote a report[49] and compiled the evidence. One of the people said, 'You just go into an organization and you can smell engagement.'"

> "In large organizations I have my own little private assessment. When I go to a large office tower and I have to wait at security for someone to come and get me, I like to watch people to see who says hello to the security guard. Who connects with the security guard? I would venture to say in a small act such as that, those people who in a small way connect with the security guard are probably more engaged. I

---

[49] http://www.bis.gov.uk/files/file52215.pdf

do not have solid business evidence of that. You can start to pick it up with the smallest of behaviors.

We influence each other. Managers and leaders have a disproportionate influence on engagement and can really start to sway and influence things as you go along.

Regardless of your role in an organization, how engaged are you? How connected are you to your work? To results? To performance? To strength? To energies? And to the moments? Then you start to look at the spread effect. Maybe rather than having more surveys, we need to have more conversations. At a certain level disengagements should not be a punishable offense; the act of disengaging should be a trigger for a conversation. 'What is going on for you?' 'What is going on with connection with the organization?' 'What is happening here that is creating that?' Good organizations are not necessarily good for everyone.

I think conversation, connection and invitation are factors that can play a huge role in what is happening. I mean it is hard to connect to a big organization. It is a little easier to connect with your supervisor, manager or other people around you.

One of the things we need to guard against and watch for is that engagement is not seen as some sort of soft skill, touchy-feely, make everybody happy kind of thing. When I look at engagement I am looking at people who are engaged in the results. They know what the organization is trying to achieve. That has been communicated by the organization. The very engaged organizations are taking people closest to the customer, and they are saying, 'Help us craft a strategy.' With the social media tools that are available today inside organizations and outside organizations, we can really give some employees an opportunity to be a part of what is going on.

Not every employee is going to take the invitation, but there are some employees that really can influence our strategies and what we are trying to achieve and what we are trying to do; because, they are seeing the customer all the time. I think we need to really look at engagement from a broader and a bigger perspective, so much to the point that eventually I hope that engagement dies, as it were, because it just gets consumed in the way we work. One of the things that really gets to me is the term 'discretionary effort.' I believe that all effort is discretionary. People can make a choice any day, whether to work or not to work. There are consequences, do not get me wrong, but there really is not such a thing as discretionary effort, or some sort of extra work. It is all discretionary.

I am trying to do what I can around the globe and on the very local level to infuse engagement into the way of work. Gather a community. I am in a global community of people who are doing things. I believe that small is not insignificant, so as opposed to big scale programs and major initiatives, I think it is what we do within the moment. My engagement changes maybe 30 or 40 times during the day. I am very engaged in this phone call. After this I might have to do some looking after bills or whatever, which might be somewhat disengaging for me.

I look at small being the new significant, and what we do in the moment to moment, as long as that small is attached to the significant. It is not just oh, 'just smile five times a day', or 'say hello to people', or 'have these little conversations', that is not what I have in mind, but if we say, 'We need to increase revenues by 20 percent to stay viable in this tourist industry, given the decline in the US economy and the lack of visitors into Canada, let us look at three or four things that we can do'. If we do that on a regular basis it may really influence revenue. If we take the customers we already have and we engage with them in a stronger way and we delineate, here are two or three things that we can do, we may make them repeat customers'.

If we talk about our organization in a positive way when we are not at work, we never know who at a party or in a situation may say, 'Hey, I have never gone up to that area. I would love to go stay at that hotel and go see what is going on and what is happening there.' I think that is why I love your idea of the guerrilla approach. The guerrilla approach is not a massive D-Day landing on the beaches of Normandy. I think it can make a difference, a huge difference."

"Negative can be okay. That can be a sign, a barometer to let us know that something is going on. Let us not shy away from that person, let us hold the conversation. 'You know three times I saw you say these kinds of things to customers. When you said those things to customers, I was thinking either you are finding customers really irritating at that point in time, or maybe there is something going on outside of work that is really having an influence. Can we just sit down for a minute or two to talk about that? I am concerned about you. I am concerned about the influence it is also having on the customers.' And my God, all of a sudden the person comes down and says well, 'My daughter has been sick, and I have not told anyone.' All of a sudden you see something different. 'I have just become really cynical of this work and what is going on and maybe we need to talk about how I make a shift or a change.'"

David and I talked about the shift from an autocratic workplace that has happened over our years as employees. David stated,

"All of us parents have that chilling situation when our four-year-old looks up at us and said, 'You are not the boss of me.' You cannot boss a four-year-old. We cannot boss people in the workplace in that old kind of command and control situation. If there is something urgent and really important, okay let us do it. If you bankrolled enough goodwill, people will probably be okay with it. I think the workplace is much more around engage, invitation, connection, collaboration, and involvement. Do not get me wrong. Those are tough, tough things for managers, supervisors, presidents and leaders to be able to operate from, because, there is already so much on their plate."

"Stephen Covey unfortunately passed away this summer and he always said 'Begin with the end in mind.' He was talking about the result we are trying to achieve. I think the other ending that he did not mention, but I think is really key, is 'What needs to end for engagement to begin?' How much can we heap onto people's plates? When I look at organizations

doing things around engagement, one of my questions for them frequently, is what are you going to stop doing? What is ending to even create enough capacity for people to do that?

You cannot just say, 'You know, now all our assistant managers in this hotel will work more on engagement,' without giving them some capacity, or giving them some skills, or giving them some input to be able to have that role. I think engagement is simple, and yet there are a number of variables that take place. I built a pyramid of engagement with ten blocks. We have got:

- *Engagement results;*
- *Engagement performance;*
- *Engagement progress;*
- *Engage with relationships;*
- *Engage with recognition;*
- *Engage with the moment;*
- *Engage with strength;*
- *Engage with meaning;*
- *Engage with wellbeing; and*
- *Engage with energy.*

That is a tall order, but when you start to bring all those blocks into play, it becomes quite powerful and paradoxically it is often very small behaviors that, if you enact, will influence all those blocks of the pyramid."

The aim of this book is to give you easy to understand principles and actionable, guerrilla marketing strategies and tools. So let us look at guerrilla employees in another way. You know a great employee when you see them, right? They are not just going through the motions to perform their duties so that they can do the minimum necessary to avoid reprimand. They are the people that are (nearly) always on. They love their work, they are a pleasure to be around, they take great care of your customers and they contribute well to your bottom line.

What can you do to increase employee engagement and your own engagement?

Little Steps Make a Big Impact

The Ka'anapali Beach Hotel[50] created a program designed to teach the staff about Hawaiian values to differentiate itself from the competition, which started with a half day workshop. Afterwards, the employees created a mission statement to reflect those values in their work. The program continued and employees participated in designing the quarterly curriculum, suggesting topics for classes and some even teaching the classes themselves.

The typical employee turnover rate at Maui hotels can reach as high as 100 percent, and poaching of employees is a concern. However, since the program started, employee retention significantly improved, with the annual turnover rate decreasing from 36.5 percent in 1985 to 9.6 percent in 2000.

Revenues at the Ka'anapali Beach Hotel were 32.5 percent lower than the average of 28 neighbor island hotels (hotels outside of Oahu) but its income was 22.9 percent higher and its occupancy rate of 90.5 percent was the highest in Ka'anapali, which averaged 85.1 percent during the same period.

As this example shows, creativity, communication, inclusion and commitment – rather than a huge budget and massive undertaking – can have a huge effect on your profits. Include your employees and give them the tools that they need to do their jobs well. Focus on the engagement of your customers, the engagement of your employees, your profit and cash-flow and your business can achieve new heights.

Rosen Hotels and Resorts Program to Engage Employees

In previous chapters I included excerpts from my interview with Harris Rosen, Founder and President of Rosen Hotels and Resorts. In this excerpt we discuss how he inspires and retains his employees.

> *"Well, it is really not very complicated, because I have been here for so long, and so many of our associates have been with us for so long. I have always set an example of working hard, and people know that I work hard. I am always very respectful to those who are part of the Rosen family of hotels and I have*

---

[50] http://www.besteducationnetwork.org/_bestCase/pdf_kanapali.pdf

always treated everyone as I would like to be treated. We were probably one of the first to offer healthcare to all of our associates along with a profit sharing program, and a multitude of other really terrific benefits including free college for staff and dependent children, free fitness, and Weight Watchers, etc. Twenty years ago we decided to build our own medical center for our associates and their dependents in order to offer the best healthcare anywhere. In fact we just completed a new medical center, which is about three times the size of the first one. Our healthcare benefit is probably the best in the industry and it may indeed be the best anywhere. If you are sick and you are in the hospital, the most you pay is $500 for the first and second visit; after that we pay all of your hospital costs.

We have never discouraged entire families to work for us, so we have lots of moms and dads and kids working for us. We, as a company, do lots of things together. Our associates are very proud of the community work we do. I think they take great pride in being associated with an organization that cares a great deal about their community. About a third of our associates are from Haiti, and we have done a lot of work in Haiti and we are about to initiate a very bold program in Haiti. We are currently planning to build our first village. Our Haitian associates love the fact that we (their company) are involved in Haiti. I think all of the things that we have done, whether it is our Tangelo Park Program or the new Jewish community center, or the UCF Rosen College of Hospitality Management or our work in Haiti, I believe our associates are very proud of what we do to help others.

If you go around the table, and ask our associates how long they have been with us, it is very unusual to find anyone who has been with us for less than 10 years. Many have been with us for 20, 25, or even 30 years or longer."

Even if you own a small business, what can you do to build a community inside your business? What can you do to build a culture that inspires engagement? What can you do to bring your employees to the table to reduce turnover, theft, absenteeism and other controllable costs while creating ways for the employees to get more done, to be able to wow their customers, to be more committed to the success of your business? Having an engaged workforce requires 100 percent commitment from leadership before you start because making the changes necessary to get the right people in the right seats, with the right attitude to succeed is not an overnight occurrence. It is a process that will require some tough choices but with all things worthwhile, a solid commitment to your plan to become a better employer will pay off handsomely as people flock to be part of something great.

Chapter 17 – Incentive Programs

"We invest in our biggest assets: our people and culture."
G.J. Hart

A couple of years ago, I was in a meeting where my friend Bob and I were talking about using incentives to change behavior. Bob warned me prior to the start of the meeting that he had to watch the clock because he had to check-in for his flight to get a good seat. As the time drew nearer, we stopped our discussion and brought up the check-in page for the Southwest Airlines website on my laptop. Bob entered the requested information and as soon as the clock hit "that time", he hit "enter" to finish the check-in. It turned out that he was the thirtieth person to check in, which was acceptable to him. Having never flown with Southwest, I had no idea that this was how the boarding was managed and I was intrigued. Bob laughed and said, "Yes, behavior can be changed. After all, when you get out of bed at 6 a.m. to go to the lobby to check-in for a flight and you meet others who are doing the same, you know it is possible." The incentive of having a good seat was so strong that Bob and these other passengers got out of bed, got dressed and waited to use the check-in computer a full 24 hours before their flight.

What Incentives are Used For

Incentives are used to inspire people to do what you want them to do, when you want them to do it. Everyone has a unique way of processing information, of responding to an offer, and making a decision to act. In the Guerrilla Selling chapter Jay Rosenberg explained marketing to personality types and how the Olympian personality responds very well to incentives and they are the first to buy. Jay explained that the Thinkers are the last to buy and they take their time to make decisions but once they have decided you can upsell and cross-sell to them. Incentives can make the initial sale or the back-end sale happen today.

Incentives Work

- The fixed cost of Incentive Programs, unlike other sales and marketing strategies, is 20 to 30% of the Program. The remaining 70 to 80% is paid ONLY when the Program's goals are reached. (Source: Incentive Research Foundation: 'Why Incentive Programs Endure Recessions,' December 2008)

- Companies with high levels of employee engagement improved their operating income by 19.2% while companies with low levels of engagement saw their operating income decline by 32.7% over a 12 month period. (Source:"FORUM - The Economic Case for People Performance Management and Measurement", December 2007.)
- 66% of employees are influenced to stay based on incentive programs (Source: Maritz 2005 poll)
- 74% of employees 18 – 34 link their future with a company to incentives (Source: Maritz 2005 poll)
- In performance improvement programs, non-cash rewards are two to three times more effective than cash rewards. (Source: Study by Scott Jeffrey, Ph.D., described in "Right Answer, Wrong Questions" Cited by Maritz)
- Incentive programs reported an 80% success rate in achieving their established goals when the correct reward was offered (Source: Incentive Federation Study)
- Executives stated that in order to achieve the same effect of incentive travel, an employee's total base compensation would need to be increased by 8.5%.(Source: The Return on Investment of U.S. Business Travel – Oxford Economics USA – Sept 2009)
- Incentive travel investments yield an ROI of more than $4:$1 (Source: The Return on Investment of U.S. Business Travel)

Properly structured incentive programs can increase performance by as much as 44 percent, but only a small number of incentive programs contain all of the elements necessary for success. (Source: Incentives, Motivation & Workplace Performance, International Society of Performance Improvement, 2002.)

Types of Incentive Programs

There are 4 main types of incentive programs:

- One-of-incentives such as you would use in fusion marketing and in promotions. Examples are discounts, value-added bonuses, special bundled pricing etc.;
- Loyalty incentives for customers such as points with purchase programs or punch cards;
- Sales incentives for employees and channel partners; and
- Non-sales incentives for employees such as for attendance, production, attention to safety, length of service and cost savings / innovation incentives.

Customer Incentives

Incentives for customers have been used for years and they typically include a value-added component, a discount or a way to accumulate "points" or some other currency for their purchases.

Loyalty programs are designed to incent customers to shop with one business instead of a competitor and they are usually based on volume of purchases. I remember that my Gran used to get stamps each time she went to the store and she would stick those stamps in her little book to save up for something special. My Mom also collected an entire set of china by shopping at Safeway. My husband, Steve, is saving up for a free car wash with a stamp card while my daughter, Lauren, earns a free slushy from the Co-Op after she buys ten and my daughter, Lindsey, buys gas from one gas station to receive a 5 cents per liter discount. Then there is my strange story: A few years ago I was one segment away from earning Elite Status with Air Canada's Aeroplan program for the following year, so I booked the shortest, cheapest flight I could in the last week of December so that I would earn the status. I actually bought a ticket to somewhere I did not have any reason to visit and I got on that plane, so I could receive the perks that came along with the Elite Status.

Loyalty points-based programs are certainly popular with consumers and businesses alike, although in recent years they have become a commodity that is less about loyalty and more about the value of the program. In other words, instead of flying with Air Canada, I now earn points from multiple sources and redeem them for flights and other rewards. My loyalty is not with the airline anymore, it is primarily with my credit card; and the only reason that I stick with this credit card is that I see value in the effort versus the reward. In my mind, that is not a loyalty program because it does not change my behavior and it does not inspire me to shop more or act on a CTA. If the Aeroplan program changes so that the value I receive is no longer there, I will change to another program.

Guerrillas know that the true value for their business is the relationship that they have with their customers and, when they create a loyalty program it is to enhance that relationship. The loyalty programs they create are simple to manage and simple to understand. The customer is loyal to the business because of the customer experience. However, when that experience includes value-added perks or special treatment or even a free slushy, car wash or coffee after they buy a certain number they will appreciate it.

One great tip from Derek Halpern of Social Triggers (http://socialtriggers.com) is to artificially enhance the progress towards earning the free product or service. Derek explains how researchers, Joseph Nunes and Xavier Drèz, discovered that cards that were artificially enhanced produced better results. Nunes and Drèz created two cards that both required eight car washes to earn a free one. The first card had eight spots and the second card had ten spots but two of them were punched as a head-start bonus. In the following nine months, 28 out of 150 people without a head-start earned a free car wash, but 51 out of 150 people with the head-start bonus earned a free car wash. The implications for tourism businesses are huge if you decide to use a punch card. Instead of creating a card that requires a specific number of purchases, create a card that has a few more spots but pre-fill them as a bonus for doing something that day. The number of purchases required is the same but the psychological impact of having a card that is on its way to being filled is enormous. In the case of the car wash, the difference was 82 percent.

Incentives for Fusion Marketing

Incentives are used with fusion marketing partners too. The incentive for the customer is an exclusive deal just for them, while the incentive to the partner could be financial or it could be reciprocal. Your offer to both the customer and the partner explains "What is in it for me?" (WIIFM) and the incentive gives them a reason to act.

Incentives for Channel Partners

Many tourism businesses rely on channel partners such as travel agents, meeting planners, incentive travel planners, OTAs, affiliates and tour operators to help sell their products. Getting and keeping the attention of channel partners is tough and so tourism companies create incentives, contests, sweepstakes and other campaigns to cut through the clutter. The incentives could be along the lines of:

- Sell five trips and earn a free trip;
- Earn five percent bonus commissions for sales made during a specific time frame;
- For every booking made this month you receive an entry into a draw for a trip (I won a trip to London in a promotion like this. I was thrilled!);
- Book a meeting this month and receive a new iPhone;
- Increase your sales by x percent this quarter and receive _____; and
- Earn x points for every dollar booked this quarter redeemable in our online catalog.

Incentives for Employees

Employees can be incented to:

- Increase sales;
- Reduce waste;
- Provide exceptional customer service;
- Increase attendance;
- Encourage cost saving suggestions;
- Aid in recruitment;
- Be more aware of safety *; and
- Length of service *,

The * items can be part of an incentive program or part of a recognition program.

An incentive program for employees sets out goals that they are to achieve within a specific future time frame in exchange for a reward. The employee then works towards achieving the goals to receive the reward offered. A recognition program (covered in the next chapter) is designed to recognize desired behavior after it has happened.

Creating an Incentive Program

In this section, the primary reference is to sales and non-sales incentives, although the best practices for creating an incentive program apply equally to all audiences: customers, fusion partners, channel partners and employees.

There are two ways to create an incentive program: the right way and the wrong way. The wrong way is more common than you may think and it usually starts with someone saying "I think we should create an incentive to _____ and I think we should give _____."

Instead, for an incentive to work properly, a series of steps need to be taken to ensure that the incentive will provide a return on investment while being appropriate and desirable to the person who will receive it. An incentive plan needs to be created, in much the same way a business plan or marketing plan needs to be created. The plan is created first, and then the programs and campaigns are developed to bring the plan to life.

Business Review – Problems and Opportunities

The correct way to create an incentive program starts with an analysis of problems and opportunities within your business. If, for example, your sales are lower than you forecasted, you need to look at the reasons why. Is it because you do not have enough products to sell? The economic climate changed? The political situation has changed? You have a new competitor? Your product quality has deteriorated? Your reputation has taken a hit? Your sales team is slacking off? You have lost a great channel partner? What is the reason?

If your sales are down because you have a new competitor, is an incentive program the right way to capture those lost sales? Maybe, but before you start, find out why you are losing to that competitor. Did they launch with a grand opening promotion that you failed to predict or is it something else?   Are they providing a better experience, a lower price, more value, a better product etc.? If you determine that your sales are down solely because this competitor is the "shiny object" that is capturing the attention of your customers, then a combination of marketing weapons as discussed in this book plus an incentive program that encourages your sales team to reconnect with customers may work for you.

If you are creating an incentive program for customers or channel partners, what is the opportunity or problem you wish to address?

Create a Strategy

Who is the best audience to participate in the incentive program to achieve your desired results?   Is it the sales team?   Operations? Customer Service? Customers? Channel Partners?

Is this going to be an ongoing incentive program or is it a short-term or one-of incentive?

What type of program will you offer? There are different types for different audiences. For example a discount, points for purchase, or punch card work for customers whereas achieving pre-defined targets work better for employees, sales teams and channel partners.

Is your program going to be open-ended, which means the program does not have a limit on qualifiers or the reward they earn?   The return on investment is generally higher with an open-ended program because there is no ceiling for the participants. The more effort they put forth, the better the results and better results yield more rewards. A closed-ended program has a predefined number of qualifiers and rewards. Close-ended programs are more common for a sweepstakes or contest.

Gap Analysis

The next step is to perform a gap analysis between corporate goals, employee performance and results. Do your employees have the skills and tools to do more than they are doing now but, for one reason or another, they are choosing not to use them to their full potential? An incentive program can work wonders when it encourages people to change their behavior in a positive way. However, get to the root of the issue. Are your employees trying to tell you things that you are ignoring? Are your rules and policies making it hard to deliver the brand promise and exceptional experiences?   Are your customers complaining about the same issues? Incentive programs are business improvement tools that work well but they cannot fix a broken business. Fix the broken parts first then incent your audience to behave in the desired manner.

Program Impact Research

If an incentive program is a viable tool to solve your problem or to capitalize on an opportunity such as launching a new product or increasing year-over-year sales, the next step is to take a look at how the incentive program you are contemplating will affect other areas of your business. If you increase sales, do you have enough capacity to handle the increase? If not, make the changes necessary before getting started.

You now know what you want to fix or launch and that an incentive program can help without negatively impacting other areas of your business.

Establish Objectives

Your next step is to create the objectives that you expect that your program will achieve. While creating your objectives be sure that you do not have short term objectives that negatively impact long-term objectives or that will conflict with your vision and mission for your business. The short term objectives of this incentive program will help you to achieve the long-term objectives of your business. The objectives should be SMART: Specific, Measurable, Attainable, Related and Timely.

Take a look at all your objectives and see if there are any that will be impacted by outside factors such as new legislation, environmental or economic factors and your competitive environment. If you create an incentive plan to increase sales, how will your competitors react? Are your objectives still valid, achievable and measurable?

Number Crunching Time

When you use incentives to achieve better results you need to understand your baseline numbers. You are going to have marketing promotions throughout the year, you may have a fusion marketing arrangement and outside factors will impact your results. You need to understand the impact the incentive program has on the results so that you know whether it was the incentive program that was responsible, or one of your other initiatives.

What results do you expect, factoring in your other initiatives and influences, if you did not institute an incentive plan? In other words, what is your current forecast? When you add an incentive plan, you do so to change the current forecast so that you have better results. What does the best case scenario look like? The worst case scenario? The most likely outcome, if you add this incentive program? For example, if your projected sales for next year are $1,000,000 without the incentive program they may be $1,750,000 best case, $1,400,000 most likely and $1,200,000 worst case. Go through your forecast and budget to factor in adjusted sales, expenses and net profit based on the best, worst and most-likely scenarios if you run the incentive program. To make it easy to follow this example, let us say that your net profit without the program is $250,000; with best case it is $437,500; most likely it is $350,000 and worst case is $300,000. This means that you have between $50,000 and $187,500 of incremental profit to spend on your incentive program ($300,000 - $250,000 = $50,000 and $437,500 - $250,000 = $187,500). You are not going to spend all of the incremental profit though, so let us take the worst case scenario and use 50 percent of that incremental profit as the initial budget to fund the program = $25,000. If you exceed your worst case scenario and you have an open-ended program structure, your rewards budget will increase because your participants (sales people in this example) will have closed more sales. That is great news.

Now that you know your budget, you need to calculate how to allocate it. Take 20 percent to cover administration, training, marketing and communications. This leaves 80 percent to cover the rewards, shipping and taxes = $20,000. Now is the moment of truth -- does the 80 percent afford you enough of a budget to create an incentive program that is "worth it" in the minds of the participants?

The rule of thumb for a sales incentive program is that the value of the incentive rewards should equal five percent of total compensation during the program period and five to ten percent of incremental sales (in this example, using the worst case scenario this would equal $10,000 - $20,000, which is right on target).

Therefore, if the program is running for three months and the salesperson will earn $36,000, the rewards offered should be at least $1,800.00, ($36,000 x 5% = $1,800). Assuming that you do not have more than 11 sales people that will qualify for the full value of the reward ($20,000 / $1,800 = 11.11) your incentive program's rewards component will be well funded.

If you are creating an incentive for a fusion marketing arrangement use your profit margin, CLV and CAC as your key budget generating numbers. If you are creating a loyalty program take a portion of your net profit. If you are creating a one-of incentive, consider your CLV and profit margin.

Set Goals for Participants

What are you expecting the participants to do? Will you have different goals for different participants? It is smart to consider ways to level the playing field, for example, if you are running a sales incentive in multiple regions, there will be differences in each region. Some regions may be experiencing growth and a strong economy, whereas others may be declining.

The reality is that your top 20 percent of sales people will qualify for the reward and the bottom 20 percent will not even try, so when you are creating your goals, think of goals that will move the middle 60 percent of your sales team because that is where you are going to get the most return.

Creating the Rules

Every incentive program has a set of rules that outline what actions / behaviors are being rewarded, how long the program is running, who can participate and how the reward will be determined. Now that you know your rewards budget of $20,000 you can calculate how to divide that up to match the objectives of the program (to increase sales by at least $200,000 but most likely $400,000).

Your participants will look at your rules to decide whether to engage with the program, so make them easy to understand, equitable and doable. Keep in mind the effect that the incentive program will have on other areas of your business and the outside influences that your participants have no control over and factor those into the rules. Be sure to include a rule that "gimmes" do not qualify, for example if a competitor goes out of business and a salesperson picks up sales by default, these sales would not qualify for the incentive program as they would have happened without any effort from the sales person. Also include a rule that says that you reserve the right to change or terminate the program at your sole discretion and be sure to get approval from your legal counsel before instituting your program. Remember, your goal is to change behavior and reward actions that will impact the business positively in the short-term and the long-term so create appropriate rules.

Select the Reward

In our example of the wrong way to create an incentive program, the reward was one of the first items that were considered. You cannot choose the reward until you know the strategy, audience, structure, objectives, rules and your budget. Now that you know these factors, your job is to find a suitable reward that will be inspiring enough to exert the effort necessary to achieve the goals set out for the participants. This is a tricky step because you need to know your audience. Do not choose a trip to Rome because you (or the boss) always wanted to go there. Think about the participants and what they would want. More often than not, they will tell you that they want cash but do not fall into this trap. Cash is confused with compensation and it becomes expected. Cash has no trophy value or bragging rights and cash has no emotional appeal. Remember that your incentive participants are no different than your customers – they want a great experience.

Reward choices can be as personalized as you want them to be. One participant, who had qualified for every incentive program and had more than enough electronics, sports equipment and trips, chose to have his daughter's private school tuition paid for as his reward. Another chose to lease a car. These were large budget incentive programs but the same can be done with smaller budgets.

Reward catalogs with many options are a popular choice because there is something for everyone at different price points, which works very well with a program that awards points for various actions (for example, sell 5 earn 500 points).

Travel, as you know being in the tourism industry, is a highly desirable reward because of the motivational impact a fantastic trip experience provides. Group travel programs typically provide elements that the participant would not / could not do on their own. Group travel programs are also desirable for competitive people, such as sales people, who like to rub shoulders with other successful people and senior leaders so that they can become more successful too. For those people who would prefer to travel with friends or family, individual travel rewards are perfect for them. They still have the emotional connection to an experiential reward while they travel on their own terms.

Gift cards and stored value cards round out the typical rewards for an employee, sales or channel partner incentive program and they have their place. However, their value is transparent and they are very close to cash.

If the incentive is a one-of incentive for a fusion marketing arrangement or a promotion to get people to buy-now, choose your reward accordingly, remembering that the CLV is what ultimately matters.

Create and Administer the Program

After doing all this preparation, the next step is to put all the pieces together to create the entire program. You will create your communications material and you will also choose how you intend to administer the program. Although it is possible to run a program using Excel spreadsheets and paper claim forms, best practices for running programs include using software to manage everything from participant registration, to communications, points tracking, points redemption and reporting. You can also outsource all components or some components to an incentive professional, which will save you time, energy and resources while you benefit from the expertise and buying power. Our incentive division, Marquee Incentives, http://marqueeincentives.com can help.

Analyze Results

During the qualification period for your incentive program it is important to monitor results. Are you seeing what you expected? Are you on track for your most-likely results? Has an outside-factor that was not expected affected the outcome? Adjust your program accordingly.

At the end of your program, look at the financial, attitudinal and behavioral results. Ask your participants what they thought of the program. Listen to their feedback. Ask others who were not included in the program how it affected them. Were there any problems during the program? Did you achieve your objectives? Is the desired behavior continuing?

Celebrate Success

At the end of the program, celebrate the success with the participants and others in your business. Thank everyone for their contribution to the success and deliver the awards promptly.

Plan Your Next Program

When you created your incentive plan back at the beginning of this chapter, you contemplated more than one program because each one brings you one step closer to your long-term objectives. Now it is time to start the preparation for the next program.

Chapter 18 – Recognition Programs

"Outstanding leaders go out of their way to boost the self esteem of their personnel. If people believe in themselves it is amazing what they can accomplish."
Sam Walton

As every parent or animal trainer knows, to get your child or animal to do what you want, you consistently and immediately correct bad behavior and you consistently and immediately celebrate good behavior, sometimes with a treat. After many attempts, the child or animal learns to stop doing what you do not want them to do and instead behaves in the way you want. In sports, when a player scores a goal the fans, teammates and coaches immediately cheer; when they miss there is a groan followed by support to try again. When playing video games, the player is consistently given feedback as he maneuvers his way through the game...points are awarded when he succeeds and he loses points or lives when he does not. At work, feedback and recognition should be just as spontaneous. When you see someone scoring their own kind of goal, cheer them on and when they miss appreciate the effort and encourage them to try again.

Recognition is one of the drivers of employee engagement. Engaged employees care more about the business, they provide a better customer experience and they contribute to increased customer engagement. Customer engagement contributes to a higher CLV, which increases your profits. A business that has a culture of recognition will generally outperform other competitors because they consistently communicate the purpose, vision and goals for the business so the employees understand how the work that they do contributes to that success. A culture of recognition builds a community within the company and as you read in the community building chapter, when you have a strong community, it supports you in your efforts to achieve your goals.

When supervisors and managers do not have the time or the skills to consistently catch people doing the right thing it leaves the employee disheartened, demoralized and can lead to disengagement. Therefore, guerrillas institute recognition programs to provide guidelines for managers and employees to help recognition become part of the corporate culture.

Recognition Program

A recognition program is similar to an incentive program because it has a strategy, objectives, rules, measurement, communication and celebration. The purpose of the program is to help build more emotional connections between people at work. As you know, when someone is emotionally attached, either as a customer or as an employee, the relationship is much more valuable and rewarding. Recognition programs can be created whether your tourism business is enormous or tiny. Each of us craves to be recognized and appreciated for our contribution to the business success.

The best practice for your recognition strategy is to identify employee behaviors that advance your business' goals and values so you can recognize and reinforce these behaviors. There should be an informal component to your strategy that identifies and recognizes individuals or teams for progress toward milestones, achieving goals, handling difficult situations, suggesting profit improving initiatives, innovation and/or projects completed. This type of recognition occurs daily and employees should be encouraged to recognize other employees (peer to peer recognition). Managers can recognize employees in many ways too using:

- A verbal thank you;
- A thank you card;
- A certificate of appreciation;
- Low cost gifts;
- Refreshments; and
- Even a banana which has morphed into one of the most prestigious awards for innovation, the Golden Banana, at Hewlett-Packard.

A Golden Banana is a strange award indeed but with all things strange there is usually a story behind it. This one is about an engineer who burst into his manager's office to announce he had solved a problem his group had been struggling with for weeks. His manager was thrilled and he quickly looked for something to give the engineer to acknowledge his achievement. Finding nothing suitable on his desk, he ended up handing the confused engineer a banana from his lunch along with hearty congratulations!

A formal recognition program has defined criteria linked to the business' values and goals, a nomination and selection process, and a ceremony where employees receive public recognition along with an award. These types of programs typically only recognize a small percentage of employees for their outstanding achievement.

One of our clients had a highly successful recognition program that included a peer-to-peer component and a manager-to-employee component with a reward. Employees used our software to fill in a form, which had the corporate values prefilled. They chose the employee they wished to nominate, chose the value that they were being recognized for and they described what the employee did. The data from the form created a certificate of appreciation which was emailed to the employee and his/her manager. The employees printed their certificates and proudly displayed them all over their workspace. There were thousands of certificates on display throughout the organization. The managers then personally recognized the employee for their effort too. If the effort was significant, the managers could take the peer nomination and reward the employee with points as a thank you for their effort. The managers also nominated employees for reasons that they identified themselves and awarded them points based on the rules of the program. The manager to employee recognition certificate was emailed to the employee and the manager followed up with a verbal thank you. On a few occasions my team was asked to override the process so that the manager could present the certificate personally, instead of having it emailed. I loved it when we were asked to do this as it put the personal touch back into the recognition. The employees redeemed their points in an online catalog and their reward was shipped within one week of being requested.

Guerrillas know that it is extremely important to know your employees so that you can recognize them appropriately. Understand what motivates your employees because each person will have different motivators. Also understand different personalities. Some people love to be publicly recognized while others prefer to be recognized in private. In some cultures, individual recognition is frowned upon but team recognition is fine. Know your employees and ask them what motivates them and what type of recognition they prefer.

For more details about the best practices for recognition programs, go to http://recognition.org which is the website for Recognition Professionals International. For more ways to reward employees, check out Bob Nelson's books which have thousands of recognition ideas.

Interview with David Zinger

In my interview with David Zinger (http://davidzinger.com) we talked about recognition and how it impacts engagement. Here are some excerpts from the interview. The entire interview is available at http://carolwain.com.

> *"In the old days recognition was somehow seen as giving people a toaster, or a long service pin, or some token. In today's age recognition is much more strategic, much more social. It resides at all kinds of different levels with that. We are failing – many organizations and many people – to recognize the people we are working with. That is why I like to watch people when they enter a large organization going by the security guard.*
>
> *Did they recognize that there is a person there? By recognition, I do not mean that they put a badge on the security person, it is, 'Hi, how are you?' 'How are the kids?' 'What is happening here?', or 'What is happening there?' That very short act of recognition tends to energize the person who receives it, and paradoxically tends to energize the person who gives it. It is like an exercise program. If you are out of shape and you go exercise, it is awful. It is taking energy to get going, but you are saying during the day, 'Oh I feel more energetic now.'*
>
> *I think the same thing happens with recognition. I see recognition a little bit deeper than some. I also look at recognizing when people are really floundering or having difficulty. Recognition to me does not always have to be 'Atta girl, way to go. Good job. Nice, I like the way you did this.' Recognition is also, 'Hey, I have seen a change in you. Three*

times in the last two days, this is what I saw. When I saw that I was thinking this or that or the other thing.' That is really powerful recognition.

The old definition of leadership or management was getting work done through others. Well, that does not fly any more. It is getting done work with others. 'With' is very different than 'through'. 'With' means that you notice and you see things. You say things. It does not have to be huge. I am not talking about big performance appraisal systems. I am just talking on a daily basis, maybe eight times or ten times, saying, 'This is what I saw, this was what I was thinking, was that going on? Is there something else happening?' That is pretty powerful.

We have a billion mobile workers now around the globe. I think we need to keep connected to those mobile workers by being able to let them know that we are aware of them, what they are doing out there. We see their work. We let them know what we are seeing in their work, or whatever; because we are not seeing them as much.

A lot of good organizations will do their best to at least get in person every so often, so that they can have that human connection. The social tools now are pretty awesome. You look at the employee engagement network, that is a public community, but you can run that internally, so that you have pictures of everyone. You are able to update what is going on, and see what is happening with people. I think managers and leaders have to work a little harder in that situation to go out and maintain that connection. Although in some ways texting can be a real nice way to communicate if it is appropriate and it works well, that may be a tool along the way.

Communication is such a chore even when we are all working in the same place. When we have people all over the map, trying to get that communication about what is our strategy? What are we trying to achieve? What are we working on? That is got to be a real strong powerful ongoing process."

Leveraging Employees

When your business is people-focused with a strong vision; strong leadership; strong relationships, strong processes and controls, and strong communication then your employees will know what to expect, how to act, why it matters, what your goals are and they know "WIIFM?"

When you have the right people in the right roles, you can leverage their efforts to achieve your goals and deliver your brand promise. Your customers receive a fantastic experience that helps them to engage with your brand. Your employees are happy that they are working in a positive, supportive and successful business where they receive regular feedback, opportunities, recognition and rewards. Most importantly, you are thrilled to have a profitable, vibrant and sustainable tourism business that serves your ideal customers with the products and services that solve their problems. That is a true guerrilla success story!

Part Four –
Action Time

In this section you create your plan to increase your profits by leveraging technology, relationships, resources and expertise.

Chapter 19 – Understanding Your Own Marketing

"Don't find customers for your products; find products for your customers."

Seth Godin

In this last part of the book, I will pull all the concepts together to help you to create an actionable plan. Grab a notebook or open a Word document and answer the questions I have asked below. You can also purchase the Guerrilla Marketing Workbook which has the questions, tables, forms and more explanation by following the link on the http://carolwain.com website.

Before Getting Started, Let us Take a Look at You

If you are an entrepreneur you have the ability to create the ideal business, with the ideals clients, the ideal lifestyle and the ideal business model. Before getting started on your marketing plan, take a few moments to become clear on your profit potential. This is a very valuable lesson, which I learned from Marie Forleo, and it is a step that many of us forget to take. You may find that you have created a business or a role within your business that does not fit your strengths or desires. If this is the case you can make the necessary changes. If you find that you have matched your talents, dreams and lifestyle to your business, fantastic. You will know that you are on the right track.

- How do you love to work with people?
- What comes so naturally to you that it does not feel like work?
- How do you love to spend your time?
- What do people say that you are good at? (Ask at least 25 people to tell you what your best traits are. I sent an email asking people to tell me the three best traits that popped into their minds, without censoring their thoughts or telling me what they think I wanted to hear. The results were very interesting.) The goal is to brainstorm ideas that call upon your key strengths.

Did you discover something about yourself that you did not know? Were there any surprise traits that people shared with you?

Show Me the Money

Let us take a look at what you are currently offering within your business. There are likely many products and services that you offer with varying degrees of profitability. Track which products and services are making you money and which ones should be changed or eliminated. You can be as detailed as you would like, the point of this exercise is to understand which products are making you the most profit and which ones need to be replaced or revamped. Here is a sample matrix that you can use:

Revenue for past _____ months				
Product	Price Point	Revenue Earned	% of total Revenue	Margin
Total Revenue				

Do the products that are contributing most to your revenue also contribute the most profit? If no, then can you increase the margin on those products? Or, can you sell more high margin products than you currently do?

Marketing Plan Preparation

1. **What Are Your Business Goals for Your Desired Lifestyle?**
   Express your business goals; in terms of the amount of profit you want each month and the number of days off each month.

   Jay is "famous" for working a three day week, every week for over 30 years. Regardless of your current situation, write down what your goals are.

   Year One
   The amount of net profit I want is $_____ per month.

I want _____ days off each month.

Year Three
The amount of net profit I want is $_____ per month.
I want _____ days off each month.

Year Five
The amount of net profit I want is $_____ per month.
I want _____ days off each month.

2. **What Are the Benefits of Doing Business With You?** This list is extremely important because you will list all the reasons why your customers will benefit by doing business with you. Be bold, be brave, stick out your chest and give it a double-fist-thump. Just brain-dump, do not edit at this point.
3. **Identify Your Competitive Advantages.** From the list you just created, there are many benefits that will also apply to your competitors. So choose the items where you are different than your competitors. This is what you will focus on in your marketing campaigns. It is your positioning and your USP.
4. **Identify Your Target Markets.** The more markets where you can target your marketing, the more profits you will earn. You may have only one target market but many of us have more than one market.
5. **What is your CLV?**
6. **What is your CAC?**
7. **What is Your Brand Promise?** Your competitive advantages help you to create your brand positioning and the goal of your brand positioning is to develop a brand promise that is unique, compelling and most of all, believable. This is crucial to understand because it will determine not only how you will market but how you will sell, how you manage client expectations, what decisions you will make when presented with a new opportunity, how you will rate yourself for achieving results, how your customers are treated and what your training program looks like. All too often, when businesses go off the rails, it is because they "forgot" about their brand promise.

A short story here should help. In Chip and Dan Heath's book, Made to Stick they tell the story about Southwest Airlines:

> "Herb Kelleher, long-time CEO of Southwest Airlines, tells a friend 'I can teach you the secret to running the airline in 30 seconds. This is it: We are THE low-fare airline. Once you understand that fact, you can make any decision about this company's future as well as I can.'
>
> 'Here's an example,' he said. 'Tracy from marketing comes into your office. She says her surveys indicate that passengers might enjoy a light entrée on the Houston to Vegas flight. All we offer is peanuts, and she thinks a nice chicken Caesar salad would be popular. What do you say?'
>
> His friend hesitated, so Kelleher responded: 'You say, Tracy, will adding that chicken Caesar salad make us THE low-fare airline from Houston to Vegas? Because if it does not help us become the unchallenged low-fare airline, we are not serving any damn chicken salad!'"

What is your positioning and what is your brand promise?

8. **What Is Your Elevator Pitch?** Imagine you got into an elevator and someone asked you what you do. In the time it takes to get to your floor you need to express yourself in a compelling, unique and intriguing way that will make them hold the door to ask you for more information. So, what do you do? What is your elevator pitch?

Marketing Plan Creation

If you have more than one product for more than one audience you can and should create one marketing plan for each.

1. **The Specific Purpose of My Marketing is to**: (start with a verb/action word. For example get people to sign up for a free consultation... that is one of ours)
2. **The Competitive Advantage I Want to Stress is:** (take this from your competitive advantage list)
3. **Our Target Audience is:**
4. **Our Ideal Customers (for This Product/Service) Are:**
5. **The Marketing Weapons We Will Use Are:**
6. **Our Niche in the Market is:**

7. **Our Identity (who you really are and what you really stand for) is:**
8. **Our Marketing Budget Will Be _____ % of Our Projected Gross Sales in Year One.**

That is it... simple, easy and did not take very long at all.

Chapter 20 – Your Guerrilla Marketing Calendars

"He who fails to plan is planning to fail"
Winston Churchill

Now that you have been introduced to a number of guerrilla marketing weapons and you have read about cross channel marketing, it is time to create your marketing calendar. As with everything "guerrilla" this is a simple exercise that you can easily do in under an hour. In fact, at Guerrilla Marketing Intensive, Jay gives us only fifteen minutes to complete this task.

Your guerrilla marketing calendar enables you to project three years into the future and it will only get more valuable as those years pass because you will track your progress and split test as you go along. Start with the first year and then you will use your results to determine years two and three.

Guerrilla Marketing Calendar

Year One

Month	Message	Media Used (List all) Note: You will create a separate detailed blog and newsletter calendar but list the items here too	Cost	Return on Investment	Results (Grade)

Create your Blog Calendar

The hardest part about blogging is in knowing what to write about each time you create a post. After defining your yearly guerrilla marketing calendar, take a look at what your message is each month and brainstorm topics that match the message. Tip: look at the frequently asked questions you receive for inspiration. Choose about 40 topics that you could cover (you will only cover one simple topic per blog post to avoid burning yourself and your readers out).

Now choose 26 topics by highlighting the best ideas. When you are done, you have 6 months worth of posts identified (assuming you post every week). Now put them in your calendar. I suggest Google Calendar for keeping all your various tasks organized.

Month	Message

Create your Newsletter Calendar

In the same way you just created your blog calendar, you should create your newsletter calendar. Remember that when you plan ahead of time, you can match your newsletter and your blog to your promotions.

Month	Message

Success! Congratulations for taking action to create your plan and your calendars. If you intend to offer a recognition program and / or incentive programs for customers, employees or partners, now would be a great time to start planning.

Next Steps

1. Visit http://carolwain.com for a list of resources and tools that can help you with your guerrilla marketing and for links to the expert interviews.
2. Goto http://guerrillatourismmarketingbook.com because there are bonuses on the site that you'll want to receive.
3. Join us on Facebook at http://facebook.com/guerrillatourismmarketing
4. Check out http://guerrillatourismmarketing.com
5. If you need help with any planning or managing any of the plans or programs discussed in this book, please email me at carol@carolwain.com.
6. You can also contact me to discuss working with you. Here are the applicable websites and a brief description of the services offered.

Carol Wain http://carolwain.com - This is where I list all the services and products that I offer, along with my latest books. Check back often as I frequently change the site, my services and products.

I currently offer coaching, training, live events and I may have room for one or two consulting contracts. You can also hire me as a speaker and workshop facilitator.

WIN-U http://carolwain.com/work-with-me/win-u/ - WIN-U is the training division of the World Incentive Network Inc. (WIN). You'll find a list of the current courses by visiting the link.

Marquee Marketing http://marqueemarketing.ca – Is my marketing agency. We help professionals, entrepreneurs and subject market experts to market and leverage their book in a way that results in "best seller status" and which elevates them above their competition. We also help authors to build and market their back-end product while positioning themselves as the celebrity and/or trusted authority in their niche.

Marquee Incentives http://marqueeincentives.com – Is my award-winning incentive company that creates incentive programs that increase profitable sales and recognition programs to drive employee engagement.

Glossary of Acronyms

AIG	American Insurance Group
BOGO	Buy one Get one
CAC	Customer Acquisition Cost
CLV	Customer Lifetime Value
CTA	Call to Action
CTR	Click Through Rate
CVB	Convention and Visitors Bureau
DM	Direct Message
DMC	Destination Management Company
DMO	Destination Marketing Organization
F&B	Food and Beverage
Fam	Familiarization trip / experience
FIT	Fully Independent Traveler
GMO	Government Marketing Organization
GSA	Government Services Administration
LBS	Location Based Services
LBS	Location Based Service
NFC	Near Field Communication

OTA	Online Travel Agency
OTO	One-time-offer / One-time-only
PPA	Pay per Action
PPC	Pay per Click
PR	Public Relations
QR	Quick Response
QSR	Quick Service Restaurant
ROI	Return on Investment
SEM	Search Engine Marketing
SEO	Search Engine Optimization
SERP	Search Engine Results Page
SMS	Short Messaging Service
TLD	Top Level Domain
USP	Unique Selling Proposition
WIIFM	What is in it for me?

About the Authors

Carol Wain

Carol Wain has been an entrepreneur since her teens with businesses that sold newspaper subscriptions, macramé plant hangers, supplements, home-party designer clothing and travel in her early days.

Today Carol sells her expertise as a coach, consultant, trainer and speaker who specializes in leveraging assets such as expertise, resources and relationships to increase revenue, profile, brand recognition and customer and employee engagement.

Specifically, Carol concentrates on joint ventures/strategic alliances, incentives, community building, customer engagement and multi-channel digital marketing along with her "Expert | Author | Celebrity" coaching and done-for-you services for experts, professionals and entrepreneurs.

With so many years of trying different things to see what works and what doesn't, she has had her fair share of great highs, devastating lows and varying degrees of success in between.

Carol built a successful incentive company around her life as a military wife and mom of two young daughters. It wasn't easy, particularly because she was living in a tiny community on the east coast of Vancouver Island, BC and she hadn't even heard of the incentive industry until she "discovered" it a few months earlier.

After devouring everything she could learn about the industry she launched her business from her living room with nothing more than a website that she created with Front Page for Dummies in one hand and an internet marketing book in the other.

Carol will never forget the day when she sold a product that netted $65,000 as it was the turning point for her business. She paid off the second mortgage and credit card bills and moved the business from the living room to the newly-renovated garage. She hired her first employee, then her second and third and they worked together there until she couldn't get house insurance any longer because revenue was too high.

After 8 years in business, she was ecstatic when she won Entrepreneur of the Year in 2003 and her life seemed perfect as she had the flexibility she needed to juggle family life and her insatiable need to travel while keeping her business a manageable size.

It was about this point when she became, in her words, "delusional" because she decided she would take the leap and implement a project she had outlined in her initial business plan. She was going to make her fortune by creating software to manage incentive programs.

Over the next 3 years, she wasted an enormous amount of cash and energy as the project failed 3 times with 3 different development teams. Then her perfect storm hit as her two best and most profitable clients declared bankruptcy in 2008 and 2009. Her employees quit one by one and she retreated to her home office and wallowed in self-pity for far too long.

Being a true entrepreneur though, she wasn't about to get a "real job" and she explored a number of options, partnerships and business opportunities before realizing that her true passion and her strength is working with successful entrepreneurs, professionals and leaders who implement her plan to improve their organizations.

Carol recognized that while well-designed incentive programs are fantastic business tools for increasing profits and nurturing relationships, there are many other unique and creative ways to leverage budgets, relationships, expertise and resources.

History repeated itself as she jumped in with both feet to learn and implement best practices for digital marketing, community building, joint ventures / strategic alliances and leveraging expertise to become a celebrity and/or trusted authority.

You can learn more from Carol by retaining her as your coach, by taking one of the courses she facilitates through WIN-U, when she speaks at events or at her workshops.

You can also join her online membership community -- specifically for small business owners, professionals and entrepreneurs -- where you'll learn how to leverage your assets along with best practices and the latest strategies and techniques to increase profit using guerrilla marketing techniques and business improvement strategies.

Originally from Scotland, Carol lives on Vancouver Island, BC with her husband and daughter. She loves traveling, boating and gardening and she is planning a great adventure to combine her multiple passions.

For more info or to reach Carol go to http://carolwain.com.

Jay Conrad Levinson

Jay Conrad Levinson is the Father of Guerrilla Marketing and the author of the "Guerrilla Marketing" series of books. Guerrilla Marketing is the best known marketing brand in history, named one of the 100 best business books ever written, with over 21 million sold. His guerrilla concepts have influenced marketing so much that his books appear in 62 languages and are required reading in MBA programs worldwide.

He was born in Detroit, raised in Chicago, graduated from the University of Colorado. His studies in Psychology led him to advertising agencies, including a Directorship at Leo Burnett in London, where he served as Creative Director. Returning to the USA, he joined J. Walter Thompson as Senior VP. Jay created and taught guerrilla marketing for ten years at the extension division of the University of California in Berkeley.

A winner of first prizes in all the media, he has been part of the creative teams that made household names of The Marlboro Man, The Pillsbury Doughboy, Allstate's good hands, United's friendly skies, the Sears Diehard battery, Morris the Cat, Mr Clean, Tony the Tiger, and the Jolly Green Giant.

After living in the San Francisco Bay Area for 35 years, Jay and Jeannie Levinson sold their home, bought an RV, towed a Jeep, and ended up, six years later, at their lakefront home outside Orlando, Florida, and close to their 26 grandchildren, their own personal DisneyWorld.

CPSIA information can be obtained at www.ICGtesting.com
Printed in the USA
LVOW07s2229060813

346586LV00027B/1220/P